EYEWITNESS GUIDES

COWBOY

Hereford cow and calf

Four quirts made of braided leather and rawhide

Canadian cowboy
wearing storm gear

Modern cowboy
on Quarter Horse

Hand-tooled
leather, A-fork
saddle, made in
Nevada, USA,
in the 1940s

Selection of
pocket watches

Old-style saddlemaker's tools

Texas cowboy
of the 1880s

Brand
mark from the
French Camargue

EYEWITNESS 👁 GUIDES
COWBOY

Old-style
leather holster
with Colt .45
revolver

Written by
DAVID H. MURDOCH

Photographed by
GEOFF BRIGHTLING

Cowgirl on
Arab horse

Three
different
silver spurs from
Spanish America

Plaited
rawhide
hobbles
from Peru

DK

DORLING KINDERSLEY
London • New York • Stuttgart

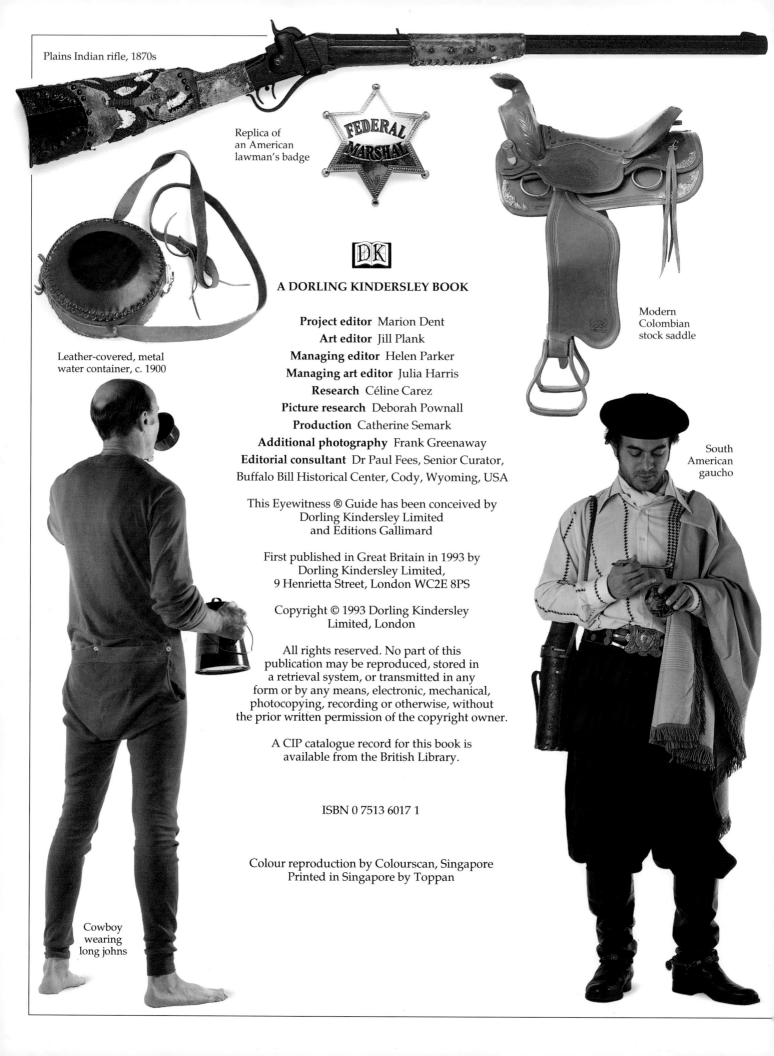

Plains Indian rifle, 1870s

Replica of
an American
lawman's badge

Leather-covered, metal
water container, c. 1900

Modern
Colombian
stock saddle

South
American
gaucho

Cowboy
wearing
long johns

DK

A DORLING KINDERSLEY BOOK

Project editor Marion Dent
Art editor Jill Plank
Managing editor Helen Parker
Managing art editor Julia Harris
Research Céline Carez
Picture research Deborah Pownall
Production Catherine Semark
Additional photography Frank Greenaway
Editorial consultant Dr Paul Fees, Senior Curator,
Buffalo Bill Historical Center, Cody, Wyoming, USA

This Eyewitness ® Guide has been conceived by
Dorling Kindersley Limited
and Editions Gallimard

First published in Great Britain in 1993 by
Dorling Kindersley Limited,
9 Henrietta Street, London WC2E 8PS

A CIP catalogue record for this book is
available from the British Library.

ISBN 0 7513 6017 1

Colour reproduction by Colourscan, Singapore
Printed in Singapore by Toppan

Contents

Well-worn
American
cowboy boots,
1920s

What is a cowboy?

THE COWBOYS OF SOUTH AMERICA
The horsemen who herded the cattle of the South American plains (pp. 48–51) bore different names – gaucho in Argentina and Uruguay, *llanero* in Venezuela, and *huaso* in Chile – but shared a love of independence.

COWBOYS WERE FRONTIERSMEN. Wherever on the world's great grasslands cattle raising began and horses ran wild, cowboys lived and worked beyond the security of settlements and the comforts of civilization. The work, attracting men who were independent and self-reliant, required courage and endurance. Cowboys, therefore, believed that their work made them different from others and took pride in their lifestyle. Sometimes the authorities and city dwellers took another view; in the USA and Argentina, cowboys and gauchos were regarded as wild and dangerous. Yet in both countries they eventually came to symbolize values which the whole nation should admire. This process has perhaps gone farthest in the USA, where the cowboy has become the centre of a myth built on the idea of the "Wild West". Hollywood has kept this myth alive, but the cowboys – and cowgirls – of Western movies (pp. 58–61) act out a fantasy which tells little of real life on the range.

ITALIAN STYLE
The Romans called those who tended their herds of cattle *buteri*. The name has survived, for in modern times the cowboy of Italy is the *buttero*. He usually rides a particular breed of horse, the Maremmana. Bred in Tuscany, in north-central Italy, the Maremmana is not very fast, but is much prized for its endurance and calm, steady temperament.

CAMARGUE GARDIANS
In the salt marshes of the Rhône delta, in southern France, live the cowboys of the Camargue (pp. 52–55). Called *gardians*, for centuries they have bred special black bulls, raised solely for fighting, and still ride the unique white horses of the region. *Gardians* remain very proud of their traditions.

A *gardian* on his Camargue white horse

NORTH AFRICAN HORSEMEN
The fierce warrior tribes of North Africa were superb horsemen. After their conversion to Islam, they began a war of conquest into Europe through Spain, but their relentless advance was finally stopped in France, A.D. 732. They rode Barb horses, famed for their endurance and remarkable speed over short distances. Barbs interbred with Spanish Andalucians (pp. 12–13), so came to influence cowboy horses throughout the New World.

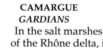

The powerful mustang – an ideal cow pony

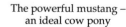

*California
A-fork style
saddle,
c. 1870*

THE FAMOUS NORTH AMERICAN COWBOY

North American cowboys (pp. 18–19) are the most famous in the world because of their imagined role in the Wild West. In reality, their work was hard, often monotonous, sometimes dangerous, and always badly paid. This, and the short heyday of the American cattle boom (1866–1887), meant most were young. Many were Anglo-Americans, though the importance of Mexican, African, and Native Americans is often ignored. Perhaps no more than 35,000 cowboys drove cattle up the trails (pp. 38–41) or rode the range.

A HARD-WORKING "HOSS"

Often the cowboy's mount was a mustang, descendant of runaway Spanish Andalucians which had bred in the wild (pp. 12–13). From the Spanish *mesteña* for horseherd, the mustang was sure-footed, tough, and fast. From 1900, wild mustangs were slaughtered for pet food until legally protected in 1970.

HUNGARY'S *CSIKOSOK*

The *puszta*, the great plain of Hungary, is home to the *csikosok*, the Hungarian cowboy. Famed for their skills as horsemen, *csikoski* are herders of both horses and the region's grey, long-horned cattle. Their dress (blue for horseherders, white for cattlemen) is traditional, as is the use of long whips.

CHARROS AND VAQUEROS

New World cattle ranching began in Mexico, the first part of the continent to be colonized by the Spaniards in the early 1500s. Land-owning *charros* and their working cowboys (pp. 8–11), the *vaqueros*, developed the skills later taken over by American cowboys. Their influence is shown by the many Spanish terms in the cowboys' work vocabulary.

*Silver
concha*

North American
cowboy wearing
batwing chaps

Charros and vaqueros

Charros sometimes imported horses from the USA, like this palomino Saddlebred, a strong breed from Kentucky, capable of covering great distances without tiring. Long, wedge-shaped leather covers on the stirrups, called *tapaderos*, prevented the rider's feet from slipping through the stirrups, being ripped by thornbrush – or bitten by the horse!

THE SPANISH SETTLERS OF MEXICO in the early 1500s brought long-horned Iberian cattle and Andalucian horses to a continent which had none. Many colonists turned to cattle ranching, a profitable as well as an "honorable" occupation, because of the great demand for hides, horn, tallow, and meat. By 1848, when Mexico lost much territory to the USA, ranching had spread to Texas and California. Rich, ranch-owning *charros* liked to display their wealth with personal ornaments of silver, much of it from the great mines at Zacatecas in northcentral Mexico. Ranching techniques spread from Mexico throughout the Americas, while horses which escaped into the wild became the mustangs of the USA and the criollos of Argentina.

Rawhide-edged leather holster, holding an expensive version of a model 1872 Colt .45, with silver butt plate and gold strap

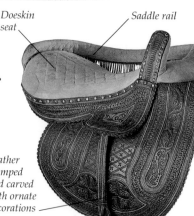

Elaborately decorated with fantastical animals and serpents

Shape of broad-armed cross

CRUCIFORM STIRRUPS
Stirrups, used in Europe from the eighth century, were essential for heavily armed riders to keep their seat, but lightly armed Asian nomads and Native Americans fought without them. These iron stirrups may have belonged to a 16th-century Spanish conqueror, or conquistador, in Mexico. Elaborately decorated, their shape echoed their rider's role as a Christian soldier of the Cross.

Classic-style tapaderos *are long and slim*

Back view of *charro* on horseback

Horn shaped like an upturned horse's hoof

Solid silver decoration on cantle

SILVER SADDLE
This magnificent *charro* saddle was made about 1870 by David Lozano, *talabarteria* (saddlemaker) of Mexico City. The artistic tooling, stitching in silver-covered thread, silver-plated conchas (decorative discs), and solid silver on the saddle horn and behind the cantle, all suggest that this was the property of a *hacendado* (a great ranch owner).

Doeskin seat

Saddle rail

Padded pommel

Silver monogram on stirrup

Heavily tooled leather showing village scenes and floral designs

Silver concha

A FINE SEAT
From the 1600s, women (condemned to wear long, heavy skirts) were able to ride only by using a sidesaddle. This late 1800s' Mexican sidesaddle has a support rail on the left, with a saddlebag below it, and a shoe stirrup on the right side. With her right foot in the stirrup, the rider crooked her left knee around the padded pommel, resting her left foot on her right knee – this is much more secure than it looks! The doeskin seat and elaborate decoration show how wealthy the owner was.

View of left-hand side

Saddlebag

Ladies' sidesaddle, Mexican, late 1800s

Leather stamped and carved with ornate decorations

View of right-hand side

Built-in shoe stirrup

TRUE CRAFTMANSHIP

British craftsmen were aware of the worldwide growth of ranching in the 1800s. This illustration – of an all-purpose Spanish-American cowboy – is from *The Saddles of all Nations*, a book published by Thomas Newton to advertise his products. Newton, who died in 1889, took over his father's lorimer business (maker of bits, spurs, and stirrups) when he was 17 and then became the first saddlemaker in Walsall, which is near Birmingham in England.

Double-skinned leather makes saddle much stronger wearing and much more expensive

Fine quality brown suede jacket and trousers

Wide-brimmed, black felt sombrero to keep sun off

Finely woven cotton scarf

Heavy cotton shirt with embroidered panels on front

Double-ear style bridle lavishly decorated with silver to match the saddle

Hand-tooled leather saddle weighs 25 kg (55 lb) and has elaborate silver decoration on horn, A-fork, and gullet

Hand-engraved silver conchas on matching breast harness

Black and white "corona", or saddle blanket

CHAMPION CHARRO

The dress and riding gear of the *charro* were both practical and a visible sign of his status. He inherited his superb horsemanship from his Spanish ancestors who accompanied early explorers, like Hernando Cortés (1485–1547), to Mexico. The men who worked on the great *haciendas*, or ranches, owned by the wealthy *charros*, were the poor *vaqueros*. A *vaquero* owned no land, probably not even a horse, but he began the noble tradition of the itinerant working cowboy, that spread from Mexico into the USA and Canada (pp. 18–19).

Mexican *charro* on a ten-year-old palomino American Saddlebred – with matching bridle, breast harness, and saddle made by the Swedish-American, Edward H. Bohlin (1895–1980), "saddlemaker to the stars" of Hollywood Westerns (pp. 60–61).

Continued on next page

Continued from previous page

Silver horseshoe

Silver thread-work in leather

A SUPERLATIVE SADDLE
This *charro* saddle (late 1800s) is finely ornamented with a silver horn, elegant bow design, and silver threads worked into the leather. The hand-tooling served a practical purpose – the friction it created helped the rider keep his seat.

Embossed silver rim on cantle

The valiant *vaqueros*

Vaqueros (from the Spanish *vaca* for cow), though from Mexico's peasantry, felt they were superior to farmers. They were proud of their work, which they believed demanded courage, fortitude, and physical endurance. In 1823, Hawaii's King Kamehameha III sent for *vaqueros* to train his men as *paniola* (cowboys). In California, New Mexico, and Texas, Mexican-American *vaqueros* formed a large and important proportion of ranch hands in the late 1800s.

Very fine Mexican saddle (late 1800s) with matching cinch (below) and spur (right)

SUNDAY-BEST CLOTHES
Formal, "Sunday-best" clothes were worn for attending church, marriages and funerals, and for fiestas. Though reflecting the climate and traditions of Mexico, they show something of their origins in 17th- and 18th-century Spain.

Silver bow design of cinch's buckle is repeated on both saddle and spur

10

Jinglebob spur, c. 1900, made by G. S. Garcia (1864–1933), a bit, spur, and saddlemaker, expert in the California style of elaborate inlaid design

Hand-tooled leather

Hand-engraved silver concha

A FINE SENSE OF STYLE
Mexican spurs often show the owner's sense of style and love of finery – these half-drop shank spurs are inlaid with silver. Attached to the rowel pins are tiny jinglebobs, which tinkle with every movement. This spur with its three silver studs shows an Islamic influence that even numbers are perfect – and unlucky!

Half-moon shape denotes Islamic origins

Silver stud

Jinglebob

A vaquero *on a Criollo*

Mexican inlaid silver spur, c. 1890

FROM BUFFALO BILL'S WILD WEST SHOW
Also inlaid with silver, these straight-shank spurs were once worn by a member of Buffalo Bill's Wild West show.

A WORKING VAQUERO
Vaqueros' working clothes varied. Some wore a plain short jacket, flared woollen trousers, and a felt sombrero (pp. 20–21). Poorer men dressed more like peasants (*peóns*), with a cloak (*serape*), cotton pants, and a straw hat.

A RICH OWNER
Such lavish and careful attention to detail suggests this spur (as well as the saddle and cinch) was the property of a man of wealth – and some vanity.

LIKE A ROOSTER'S FOOT
Prick spurs, shaped like the spur claw of a fighting cock, were less common than rowel spurs.

Mexican prick spur showing its Moorish influence

An 8-point, straight-shank rowel spur

Spur measures 14 cm (5.5 in) long

"Niello" inlay, made by silver wire hammered into the steel

ASSORTED QUIRTS
Mexican quirts (from the Spanish *cuerta* for whip) were made from plaited rawhide. The wooden grip might be filled with lead shot in order to beat down a rearing horse or restrain an untamed one when breaking it.

Mexican quirt, c. 1900

Latigo leather thong

Plaited rawhide

ROUGH RIDERS OF THE WORLD
William "Buffalo Bill" Cody (1846–1917) – buffalo hunter, scout, actor, dime novel hero – formed the first Wild West show in 1883 (pp. 60–61) and toured the USA and Europe for over 30 years. One act, "Rough Riders of the World", featured many kinds of horsemen, including *vaqueros* (left above).

IT'S A CINCH
This cinch (from the Spanish *cincha* for saddle girth) matches the saddle and spur (far left and above). It is made from fine, cream cotton cord and the dangling pieces are "shoo flies" – which are meant to do exactly what the name suggests.

Cinch made of fine, cream cotton cord

Blue and cream shoo fly made of fine wool

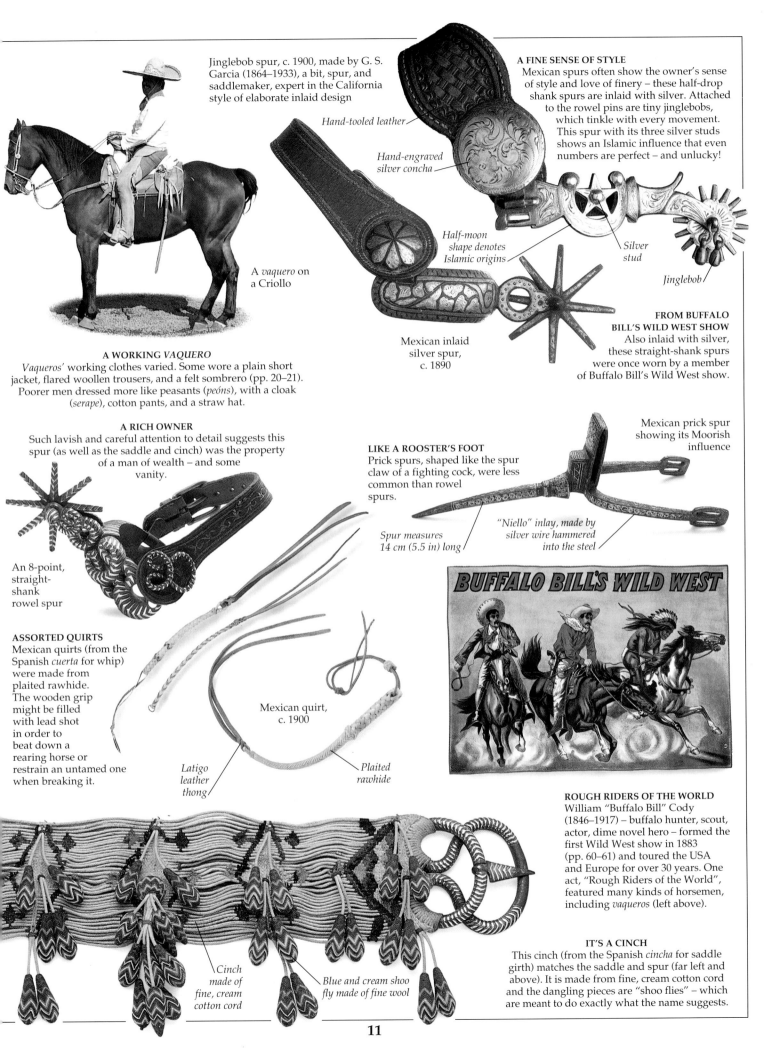

The best horses

HORSES AND PEOPLE HAVE WORKED TOGETHER since wild horses were first domesticated, probably in eastern Europe 4,000 years ago. Horses changed the direction of human history. They allowed whole nomadic cultures to range across continents. As chariot pullers and then cavalry mounts, horses transformed warfare, were the tractors of pre-modern agriculture, and were essential to any kind of large-scale cattle-raising. Wild horses died out, except for the Przewalski. All present day horses around the world are descended from these original, domesticated animals and form one species – *Equus caballus*. Environment and cross-breeding have created many variations, with different abilities, sizes, colours, and characteristics.

Built-in saddlebag

"TURN HIM LOOSE, BILL"
This painting by Frederic Remington (pp. 26–27) shows a cowboy "breaking" an untamed horse. After getting the horse used to a hackamore, or training bridle, and saddle, cowboys tried to ride the bucking animal to a standstill, in order to break its resistance. The cruel use of quirt and spurs was common.

EASTERN COWBOY
The conquering horde of Genghis Khan (?1162–1227), which created an empire from China west to the Black Sea, rode shaggy, Mongol ponies. Kazakh herdsmen in northwest China still ride these animals' descendants.

THE GAUCHOS' COW PONY
Like the mustang of the north, the Criollo is descended from feral Andalucians (pp. 8–9) which wandered into South America from Mexico. Strong, agile, and sure-footed, in Argentina it became the cow pony of the gauchos (pp. 48–51) – the cowboys of the pampas. Crossed with Thoroughbreds, Criollos produced the famous Argentinian polo ponies.

Flank cinch is loose, so that slack is taken up when roped calf pulls on lariat attached to saddle horn

A TEXAS COW PONY
This Texas cowboy, c. 1885, is riding a mustang. Both Native Americans and cowboys used mustangs, descendants of 15th-century Andalucians which had escaped and multiplied across the North American plains. Though small, the cow pony had great endurance and was hard-working.

THE FIRST AMERICAN BREED
Settlers in 17th-century Virginia in the USA crossed their English horses with Spanish (Andalucian) stock to produce the Quarter Horse – the first American breed. Named for the popular colonial sport of quarter-mile races, the Quarter Horse could produce an extraordinary burst of speed. Combined with its balance, agility, and great strength, this made the breed an ideal cow pony.

Horn secures lariat once a wild horse or calf has been lassoed

Headstall made of braided rawhide

Breast collar

"Joe's Fancy Freckle", a 6-year-old, female Quarter Horse, 14.3 hands high – a hand measures 10.16 cm (4 in) at the withers

CREAM OF THE CAMARGUE
Perhaps descended from the Asian mounts of the Huns who invaded Europe in A.D. 300–400, these white horses breed wild in the marshes of the Camargue (pp. 52–55) in southern France.

Camargue of France

A "HUNGARY" HORSE
Descended from a 19th-century Norman (French) stallion, the Hungarian Nonius was developed by mating offspring with several other breeds. Though not fast, it is a tough, reliable animal for all-round use.

Nonius of Hungary

ANCIENT ANDALUCIAN
A very old breed from the south of Spain, the Andalucian was taken by the conquistadors to the New World in the early 1600s. Its great qualities are strength and endurance.

Andalucian of Spain

PORTUGUESE PONY
Similar to the Andalucian, the Lusitano of Portugal was once prized as a cavalry horse. Its courage and agility make it the ideal choice for the bullfighters of Portugal.

Lusitano of Portugal

BELL FOR A "BELL MARE"
Just as bells are still put around the necks of lead bulls or cows in the French Camargue (pp. 52–55), bells used to be put on lead, or bell, mares in North America. The bell helped to locate a herd of grazing horses and to keep them from wandering off.

COSSACK WARRIORS
The Cossack warrior tribes of Russia were outstanding horsemen who made formidable light cavalry, first as enemies of the expanding Czarist Empire, then from the 1800s as part of the Imperial Army. Their Don horses, bred on the Russian steppes, were amazingly hardy, able to survive on the poorest foodstuffs.

Saddles – old and new

A COWBOY SAT ON HIS HORSE for up to 15 hours a day – he did not sit behind a steering wheel or at an office desk. His saddle was, therefore, his most important piece of equipment. Unlike his horse (pp. 12–13), which would probably be one of several loaned to him by the rancher, his saddle was his own and cost at least a month's wages – but it would last 30 years. Cowboy saddles evolved from the 16th-century Spanish war saddle, with its high pommel (combination of horn and fork at the front) and cantle (the raised part of the seat at the back) to hold its armoured rider in place. Over time they changed in weight and shape, but all were built on a wooden frame (pp. 16–17) covered with wet rawhide, which made the frame rigid as it dried, then recovered with dressed leather.

AN OLD TEXAS SADDLE
This 1850s' Texas saddle had a thick horn for heavy roping and fenders to keep horse sweat off the rider's legs.

A-fork frame

Short skirt

AN A-FORK
This 1870s' California saddle has an A-fork frame (from its shape), a slim horn, and steam-bent wooden stirrups. Lighter than Texas or Denver saddles, it burdened the horse less.

HIGH POINT
The Denver saddle (c. 1890) was longer than the one from Texas (top), with more leather covering. Cowboys liked the solid seat it gave, but its length and weight (18 kg, or 40 lb) sometimes gave the horse back sores.

FROM OLD MEXICO
This battered Mexican saddle shows the link with 16th-century warriors' saddles. The horn and cantle are carved wood and the simple frame is covered with tooled leather.

Cantle at back of saddle

Carved wooden horn at front of saddle

Mexican saddle, made of leather and wood

CUTTING SADDLE
This 1890s' Canadian stock saddle, for cutting out and rope work, is double-cinched. The flank (rear) cinch is kept loose, so the strain on the saddle-horn from a roped cow will pull the saddle forward and signal the horse to stop (pp. 34–35).

Front cinch

Flank strap, or cinch

ONE FROM THE NORTH
After the 1870s, saddles from the northern ranges of Montana and Wyoming brought the leather up over the horn and favoured square skirts.

Cantle

Pommel

TOUGH TAPS
Taps (from the Spanish *tapaderos*, pp. 8–11) fitted over the stirrup and gave the rider's foot extra protection from thornbrush and from rain and snow in winter. The two pairs above were called "hawg's snout" from their pig's-nose shape; the pair on the right is in the "eagle's beak" style.

Hooded 1920s' taps made from very strong cowhide leather

Stamped cowhide 1970s' taps with sheepskin lining for extra warmth

Taps (1890s) from Buffalo Bill's Wild West show

CAMARGUE STYLE
A Camargue *gardian's* saddle (pp. 52–55) has a curved cantle, a broad, solid pommel, and metal, cage-shaped stirrups. Below the pommel, always on the left, is tied his *seden* (rope).

14

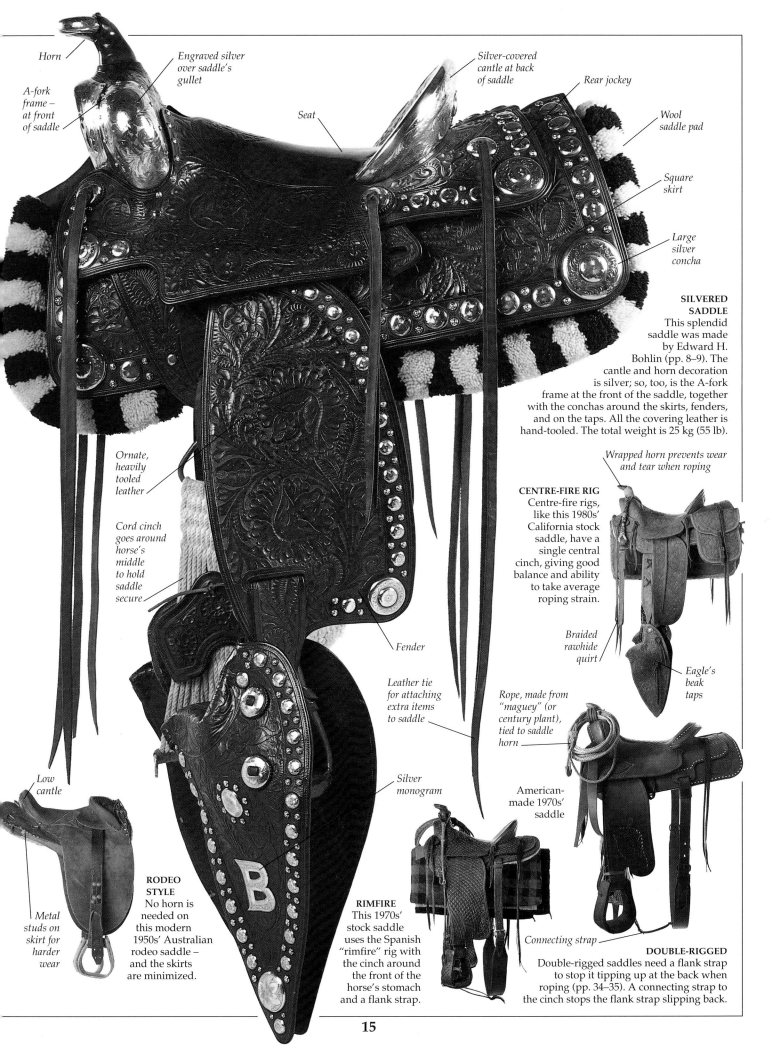

Horn

Engraved silver over saddle's gullet

A-fork frame – at front of saddle

Seat

Silver-covered cantle at back of saddle

Rear jockey

Wool saddle pad

Square skirt

Large silver concha

SILVERED SADDLE
This splendid saddle was made by Edward H. Bohlin (pp. 8–9). The cantle and horn decoration is silver; so, too, is the A-fork frame at the front of the saddle, together with the conchas around the skirts, fenders, and on the taps. All the covering leather is hand-tooled. The total weight is 25 kg (55 lb).

Wrapped horn prevents wear and tear when roping

CENTRE-FIRE RIG
Centre-fire rigs, like this 1980s' California stock saddle, have a single central cinch, giving good balance and ability to take average roping strain.

Ornate, heavily tooled leather

Cord cinch goes around horse's middle to hold saddle secure

Braided rawhide quirt

Eagle's beak taps

Fender

Leather tie for attaching extra items to saddle

Rope, made from "maguey" (or century plant), tied to saddle horn

American-made 1970s' saddle

Low cantle

Silver monogram

Metal studs on skirt for harder wear

RODEO STYLE
No horn is needed on this modern 1950s' Australian rodeo saddle – and the skirts are minimized.

RIMFIRE
This 1970s' stock saddle uses the Spanish "rimfire" rig with the cinch around the front of the horse's stomach and a flank strap.

Connecting strap

DOUBLE-RIGGED
Double-rigged saddles need a flank strap to stop it tipping up at the back when roping (pp. 34–35). A connecting strap to the cinch stops the flank strap slipping back.

15

Saddling a horse

Split-ear bridle

SITTING SECURELY ON AN ANIMAL over 1.6 m (5 ft) high, and able to control it, the cowboy was the inheritor of age-old horse knowledge. Bridles were in use by the Egyptians in 1600 B.C., though horse riders sat on pads or cloths until the saddle was invented around A.D. 350. Stirrups were first used by the Huns a century later. In the 16th century, Spanish cavalry was the finest and best equipped in Europe and Spaniards took their skills with them to the Americas. American cowboys later took over this knowledge and then adapted it. The cowboy's saddle (pp. 14–15) was a work platform on which he also had to carry his equipment. The bridle was designed to check the horse with the slightest pull on the reins.

Raised plate

Slobber chain

Half moon

A MARMALUKE BIT
The Marmaluke, like the old-style Spanish-American spade bit, had a raised plate that lay across the horse's tongue. Only the gentlest touch was used on the reins, so as not to cause the horse pain. Reins were attached to the "slobber chains" so the horse did not soak the leather.

1 ON WITH THE BRIDLE
Without a bridle, a horse cannot be controlled, so this is put on first. It comprises a bit and a headstall (split to go around the horse's ears) to hold it in place. The bit is a metal bar resting forward in the horse's mouth, so that the horse cannot get the bit between his teeth and bolt!

Maul

Spokeshave

Strap cutter

Bag of shot

Crescent knife

TOOLS OF THE TRADE
Saddlemaker's tools are simple. The strap cutter adjusts for cutting different widths of leather. The heavy maul, or hammer, is padded to prevent damage to the leather. Like the carpenter's tool, the spokeshave planes curves. The bag of shot holds down the leather without marking it, while the crescent knife allows a firm grip when cutting out curves in leather.

Fork   *Horn*   *Cantle*

Leather skirt

Rigging ring to attach front cinch to saddle

Second skin, or layer, of leather added

Basic wooden tree with several coats of lacquer

START WITH A WOODEN TREE
Made from straight-grained, knot-free pine, the tree has the metal horn screwed to the fork. It is then covered in wet rawhide, which is dried at a controlled temperature, then given several coats of waterproof lacquer.

THE BUILDUP
The saddle is built up with a series of coverings beginning with the horn, then the underside of the fork, the seat, fork, cantle, and skirts. Different thicknesses of leather are used, each shaped, then stitched with damp rawhide.

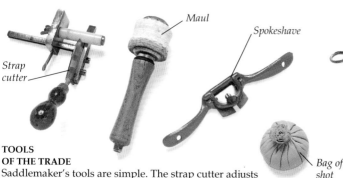

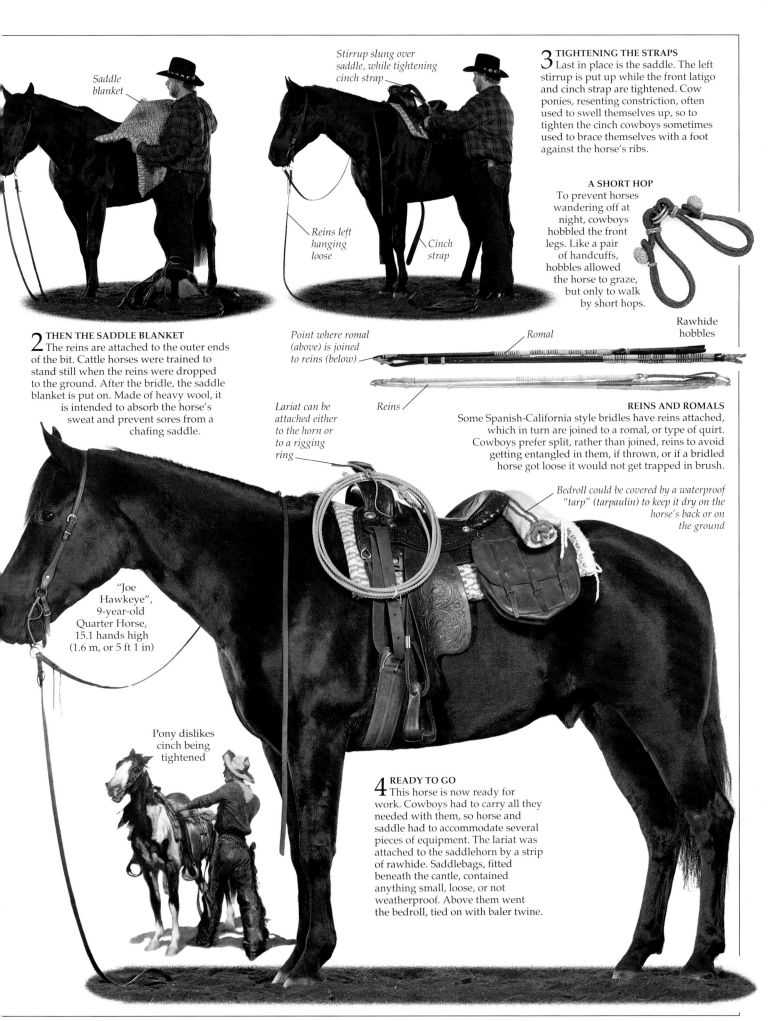

Saddle blanket

Stirrup slung over saddle, while tightening cinch strap

3 TIGHTENING THE STRAPS
Last in place is the saddle. The left stirrup is put up while the front latigo and cinch strap are tightened. Cow ponies, resenting constriction, often used to swell themselves up, so to tighten the cinch cowboys sometimes used to brace themselves with a foot against the horse's ribs.

Reins left hanging loose

Cinch strap

A SHORT HOP
To prevent horses wandering off at night, cowboys hobbled the front legs. Like a pair of handcuffs, hobbles allowed the horse to graze, but only to walk by short hops.

Rawhide hobbles

2 THEN THE SADDLE BLANKET
The reins are attached to the outer ends of the bit. Cattle horses were trained to stand still when the reins were dropped to the ground. After the bridle, the saddle blanket is put on. Made of heavy wool, it is intended to absorb the horse's sweat and prevent sores from a chafing saddle.

Point where romal (above) is joined to reins (below)

Romal

Reins

Lariat can be attached either to the horn or to a rigging ring

REINS AND ROMALS
Some Spanish-California style bridles have reins attached, which in turn are joined to a romal, or type of quirt. Cowboys prefer split, rather than joined, reins to avoid getting entangled in them, if thrown, or if a bridled horse got loose it would not get trapped in brush.

Bedroll could be covered by a waterproof "tarp" (tarpaulin) to keep it dry on the horse's back or on the ground

"Joe Hawkeye", 9-year-old Quarter Horse, 15.1 hands high (1.6 m, or 5 ft 1 in)

Pony dislikes cinch being tightened

4 READY TO GO
This horse is now ready for work. Cowboys had to carry all they needed with them, so horse and saddle had to accommodate several pieces of equipment. The lariat was attached to the saddlehorn by a strip of rawhide. Saddlebags, fitted beneath the cantle, contained anything small, loose, or not weatherproof. Above them went the bedroll, tied on with baler twine.

North American cowboys

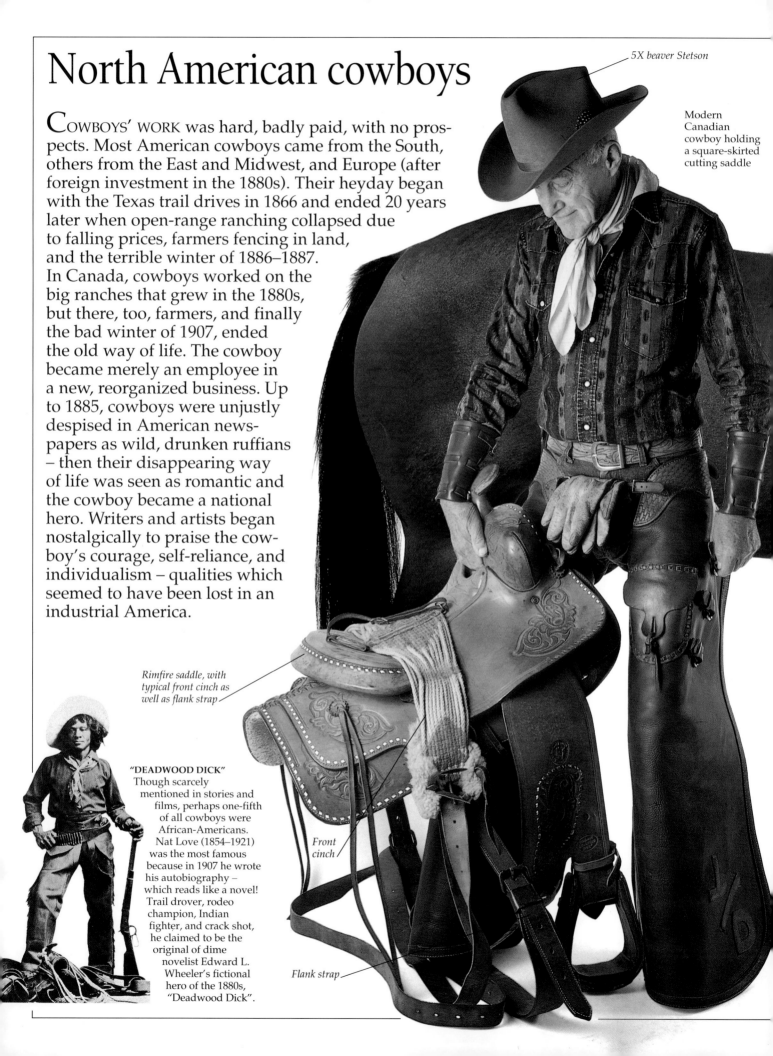

Cowboys' work was hard, badly paid, with no prospects. Most American cowboys came from the South, others from the East and Midwest, and Europe (after foreign investment in the 1880s). Their heyday began with the Texas trail drives in 1866 and ended 20 years later when open-range ranching collapsed due to falling prices, farmers fencing in land, and the terrible winter of 1886–1887. In Canada, cowboys worked on the big ranches that grew in the 1880s, but there, too, farmers, and finally the bad winter of 1907, ended the old way of life. The cowboy became merely an employee in a new, reorganized business. Up to 1885, cowboys were unjustly despised in American newspapers as wild, drunken ruffians – then their disappearing way of life was seen as romantic and the cowboy became a national hero. Writers and artists began nostalgically to praise the cowboy's courage, self-reliance, and individualism – qualities which seemed to have been lost in an industrial America.

5X beaver Stetson

Modern Canadian cowboy holding a square-skirted cutting saddle

Rimfire saddle, with typical front cinch as well as flank strap

"DEADWOOD DICK"
Though scarcely mentioned in stories and films, perhaps one-fifth of all cowboys were African-Americans. Nat Love (1854–1921) was the most famous because in 1907 he wrote his autobiography – which reads like a novel! Trail drover, rodeo champion, Indian fighter, and crack shot, he claimed to be the original of dime novelist Edward L. Wheeler's fictional hero of the 1880s, "Deadwood Dick".

Front cinch

Flank strap

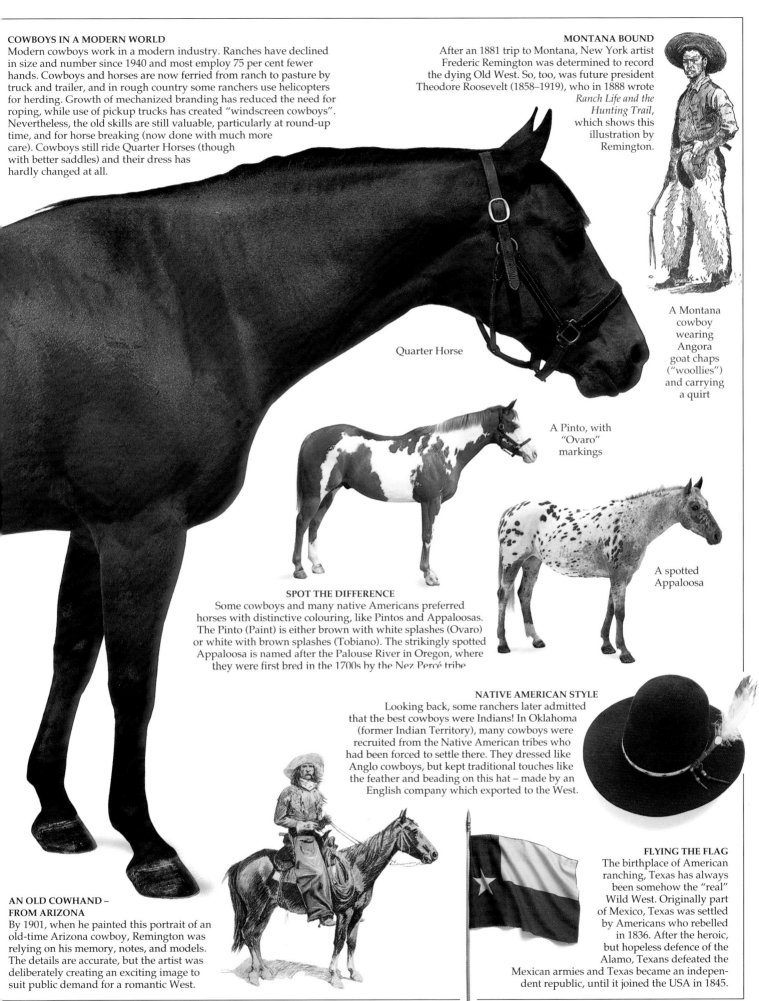

COWBOYS IN A MODERN WORLD

Modern cowboys work in a modern industry. Ranches have declined in size and number since 1940 and most employ 75 per cent fewer hands. Cowboys and horses are now ferried from ranch to pasture by truck and trailer, and in rough country some ranchers use helicopters for herding. Growth of mechanized branding has reduced the need for roping, while use of pickup trucks has created "windscreen cowboys". Nevertheless, the old skills are still valuable, particularly at round-up time, and for horse breaking (now done with much more care). Cowboys still ride Quarter Horses (though with better saddles) and their dress has hardly changed at all.

MONTANA BOUND

After an 1881 trip to Montana, New York artist Frederic Remington was determined to record the dying Old West. So, too, was future president Theodore Roosevelt (1858–1919), who in 1888 wrote *Ranch Life and the Hunting Trail*, which shows this illustration by Remington.

A Montana cowboy wearing Angora goat chaps ("woollies") and carrying a quirt

Quarter Horse

A Pinto, with "Ovaro" markings

A spotted Appaloosa

SPOT THE DIFFERENCE

Some cowboys and many native Americans preferred horses with distinctive colouring, like Pintos and Appaloosas. The Pinto (Paint) is either brown with white splashes (Ovaro) or white with brown splashes (Tobiano). The strikingly spotted Appaloosa is named after the Palouse River in Oregon, where they were first bred in the 1700s by the Nez Percé tribe.

NATIVE AMERICAN STYLE

Looking back, some ranchers later admitted that the best cowboys were Indians! In Oklahoma (former Indian Territory), many cowboys were recruited from the Native American tribes who had been forced to settle there. They dressed like Anglo cowboys, but kept traditional touches like the feather and beading on this hat – made by an English company which exported to the West.

AN OLD COWHAND – FROM ARIZONA

By 1901, when he painted this portrait of an old-time Arizona cowboy, Remington was relying on his memory, notes, and models. The details are accurate, but the artist was deliberately creating an exciting image to suit public demand for a romantic West.

FLYING THE FLAG

The birthplace of American ranching, Texas has always been somehow the "real" Wild West. Originally part of Mexico, Texas was settled by Americans who rebelled in 1836. After the heroic, but hopeless defence of the Alamo, Texans defeated the Mexican armies and Texas became an independent republic, until it joined the USA in 1845.

Hats and more hats

A COWBOY'S HAT was his trademark. Styles might vary – from sombreros to Stetsons – but the functions were the same. In blazing sun, the high crown kept the head cool while the broad brim shaded the eyes and neck. In rain and snow the hat was a mini-umbrella; it also protected against thorns and low-hanging branches. Made of high quality felt, it was meant to take years of wear. This was just as well, because a cowboy used his versatile hat as an alternative to a quirt (pp. 10–11), to carry water (as shown in the famous Stetson label), fan fires (or put them out), and occasionally even as a pillow.

Australian akubra

Gardian's hat

TWO HATS
Because they meet the same needs, around the world cowboys' hats look remarkably similar. The distinctive Australian akubra is worn all over the outback and parti-cularly by stockmen (pp. 56–57). From the French Camargue is a modern *gardian's* hat (pp. 52–55).

the last drop from his STETSON

FAMOUS LABEL
After 1885, Stetson hats (with the famous label) were worn by most Westerners. By 1906, the company was selling two million per year.

FILM STAR'S HAT
Roy Rogers streng-thened the "good guy" tradition by always wearing a white hat.

Braided decoration embroidered with gold wire meant its owner was wealthy

Hat-band made of rope

MEXICAN HAT DANCE
This elegant pre-1870s' Mexican felt hat is decorated with gold wire embroidery. Its very broad brim, braided-horsehair band, and tall crown (called a "sugarloaf" because of its shape) make it a sombrero (from the Spanish *sombra* for shade).

A SOU'WESTER?
The low-crown Plainsman's hat with a floppy brim was an alternative to the sombrero in Mexico and widely worn by cowboys in the southwestern USA up to the 1880s.

Hat-band made from broken plaited rein

Wide-brimmed, black Stetson, c. 1900

"TWENTY GALLON TENDERFOOT"
Bob Hope (b. 1903) in *Son of Paleface* wears a double ten gallon hat as a "tenderfoot" pretending to be a Westerner.

5X Beaver, Tom Mix-style Stetson

A FAMILY OF HATTERS
Englishman John B. Stetson (1830–1906) learned about Westerners' needs while gold prospecting in Colorado. From a family of hatters, he opened a factory in Philadelphia, Pennsylvania, USA in 1865 and soon produced the design that became famous – and made him a multi-millionaire.

TOP HAT
A high-crowned hat was nicknamed the "ten gallon" hat. This double ten gallon hat should earn its wearer some stares!

FILM STAR
In 1925, the Stetson company named a hat for cowboy film star Tom Mix (pp. 60–61). It had a 19.5-cm (7.5-in) crown and 13-cm (5-in) brim.

Stiff brim

Brim bound with leather

MODERN STETSON
Today's Stetsons meet the modern preference for a lower crown. This one is top quality and water-resistant, creased in the Cattleman's style. The number next to the "X" denotes the quality of the hat's material – the higher the number, the better the quality.

Best quality 10X Beaver Stetson

A HANDSOME HAT
Stetsons never had any decoration, except for a fancy hatband, perhaps. Mexican sombreros, however, were often ornamented – this one has suede appliqué and leather tassels.

Horsehair tassel

HOOKED ON HATS
In the Old West, it was not considered impolite to wear one's hat in the house. However, if provided, a hatstand might well make good use of horns and hide.

NOT SO PLAIN PLAINSMAN
The Plainsman's style had more expensive versions, such as this Mexican hat, c. 1900, made of suede with appliqué ribbon trim.

WEAR AND TEAR!
This Mexican hat has seen some hard wear. Dating from the early 1900s, it was probably the working headgear of a *vaquero*. It also looks like those which Hollywood always insisted bandits wore in silent Westerns!

STRAW SOMBRERO
Less durable, but less expensive than felt hats, Mexican sombreros might be made of straw – like this one, c. 1900.

LUCKY LUKE
The invention of French cartoonist "Morris" (Maurice de Bevère), Lucky Luke has been cheerfully cleaning up the West since 1946. He still rides Jolly Jumper and hums "I'm a poor lonesome cowboy. . .".

Dressing a cowboy

A COWBOY WOULD CHOOSE HIS CLOTHES and equipment to cope with the often brutally hard work, the country, and the climate. Clothing had to be strong enough to withstand wear and tear from working with animals at close quarters, amid spiky vegetation. It had to deal with scorching hot days and freezing cold nights. Local conditions and local customs created different styles of cowboy dress in the USA, between areas like Texas and New Mexico in the southwest, and Wyoming, Montana, and the Dakotas in the north. Revolvers were supposed to be necessary to deal with threats both animal and human, but some cowboys could not afford them – a new Colt could cost almost a month's wages. Northern ranchers tried to discourage their cowhands from carrying guns. Cowboys also followed fashion – one old ranch-hand confessed that high-heeled boots were worn out of vanity, not necessity!

Colt .45 in a leather holster

HIGH-RIDER HOLSTER
Common through the 1870s and 1880s was the "high-rider" holster which was fitted over the belt, so that the gun rested high on the hip. The cutaway for the trigger guard, as well as practice, helped a fast draw.

Convenience flap

ON TIME
Pocket watches were more ornamental than useful – cowboys would keep them in their bedroll rather than risk breaking or losing them while working. A "one-dollar railroad watch" (top) was usually a retirement present to a railroad worker, but was also sold in town stores. Gold- and silver-plated watches (below) could be bought from Montgomery Ward or Sears & Roebuck mail order catalogues (pp. 28–29) and carried a 20-year guarantee.

Silver-plated railroad watch

Plain gold-plated watch

Silver-plated with floral engraving

1 STARTING THE DAY
Day began with coffee, made from beans probably crushed between two rocks, and was drunk black, without sugar. At work, cowboys rarely took off their one-piece "long johns" – the convenience flap at the back removed the only necessity to do so! Usually made of red wool, long johns provided insulation during cold nights. Of more importance, in the heat of the day, they absorbed sweat which otherwise would quickly rot a shirt.

Long johns were made usually of red wool

Lace and buckle fastenings

Early 1900s' cuffs from California

ALL SORTS OF CUFFS
When using their lariat, cowboys usually wore gloves, made of buckskin, to avoid rope burns. From the early 1900s, they also wore stiff leather cuffs, from 13–18 cm (5–7 in) long, sometimes with a strap or laces to tighten them. Cuffs both protected the wrists and also trapped loose shirt-sleeves. Saddlers catered to cowboy vanity by stamping various designs into the leather.

Four sets of cuffs, showing both decorations and fastenings

Snap and lace fastenings

Stamped leather decoration

Basket-stamped leather

2 THE NEXT STEP

Shirt and pants were made of hard-wearing, heavy wool. Tight-buckled leather belts risked internal injury to a rider on a bucking horse. So this cowboy is wearing a pair of ex-Cavalry braces, or suspenders, though many cowboys did not like such "galluses".

3 ALL SET TO GO

Ready for work, the cowboy has knotted his bandana (cotton neckcloth), which protects his neck from the sun and acts as a mask against dust. He is also wearing a Mexican-style waistcoat. High-top working boots, with a sloped 5-cm (2-in) heel and rowel spurs, stovepipe chaps, and a high-crowned Stetson complete his outfit.

Sterling silver belt buckles from California

COWBOY JEWELLERY

Generally, a belt buckle was the only decoration a cowboy would wear. Buckles did not become popular until the 1920s, when they were given out as prizes in rodeos (pp. 62–63). These were often made of precious metals, such as gold and sterling silver, and even included jewels like rubies or diamonds.

Modern copy of old-style, high-crowned Stetson

Hat-band made of plaited leather reins

Heavy woollen shirt

Printed cotton bandana

Saddle blanket

Ex-military braces, or suspenders

Gunbelt worn loose not for a fast draw but for safety, to prevent buckle digging into waist

Striped Mexican-style waistcoat

Pin-striped woollen trousers

1850s' Texas saddle

Fringed leather shotgun chaps with front pockets

Old-style high-rider holster made of basket-weave leather

Rowel spur

Stovepipe boots

Texas cowboy of the late 1800s

Wooden stirrups are enclosed within the tapaderos

Boots and spurs

Brass spur, with buffalo head, Texas, USA, 1914

Chap hook

Iron spur from South America, 1860s

Heel chain secures spur to boot

Steel trail spur from Texas, USA, c. 1900

SPURRED ON!
Rowels on spurs were not intended to harm the horse, but to penetrate matted hair so it could feel the prod. A chap hook was an integral part of the metal shank to stop chaps or trousers catching on the rowel.

COWBOYS TOOK CARE CHOOSING THEIR BOOTS – in the 1880s, custom-made boots cost $15, half a month's wages. The high, tapered heel ensured the boot would not slip through the stirrup and could be dug into the ground when roping on foot (pp. 34–35). Western boots have remained popular, though their shape and style have changed a good deal. Today, many are not work boots, but fashion items (pp. 60–61). Because cowboys rarely groomed their horses, spurs were needed to penetrate a horse's matted hair, though rowels were usually filed blunt.

Inlaid brand mark

Vamp (top of foot) made of shark skin

Silver concha

BIG EARS
The mule ears on these boots go from the top edge to overlap the heel.

BOOTS FOR BUCKAROOS
Tall so they can be worn with *armitas* (pp. 26–27), there are finger holes for pulling boots on.

STOVEPIPE STYLE
Old-style "stovepipe" boots came up close to the knee to offer more protection. This pair dates from the 1880s or 1890s. The extreme underslung heel was just a fashion and must have made walking painful – as well as potentially dangerous!

Mexican inlaid silver spur

American, silver-plated, hand-forged spur

Neck of spur in form of female figure – in Western spurs called a "gal-leg"

Plain nickel working spur

Diameter is 9 cm (3.5 in)

South American brass spur

Spanish American, hand-forged, bronze prick spur

HISTORICAL SPURS
Spurs were brought to the Americas by Spanish settlers in the 1500s. Typically, they were large and heavy, with a traditional use of silver, mixed with iron, to create highly decorative spurs of great elegance. This Mexican style evolved in Texas, USA, and went north along the cattle trails to Kansas, Wyoming, and Montana (pp. 38–39).

SHORT AND SCALLOPED
The shorter boot with scalloped top is a modern style, probably deriving from the kind specially designed for early movie cowboys (pp. 60–61), like Tom Mix (1880–1940). These store-bought boots were made by Tony Lama of El Paso, Texas, USA in the 1970s.
A former champion rodeo cowboy, Lama opened a boot factory on his retirement and his products have become famous.

Curved tip at end of 17-cm (6.25-in) long spur

Spanish American, hand-forged, engraved, iron prick spur

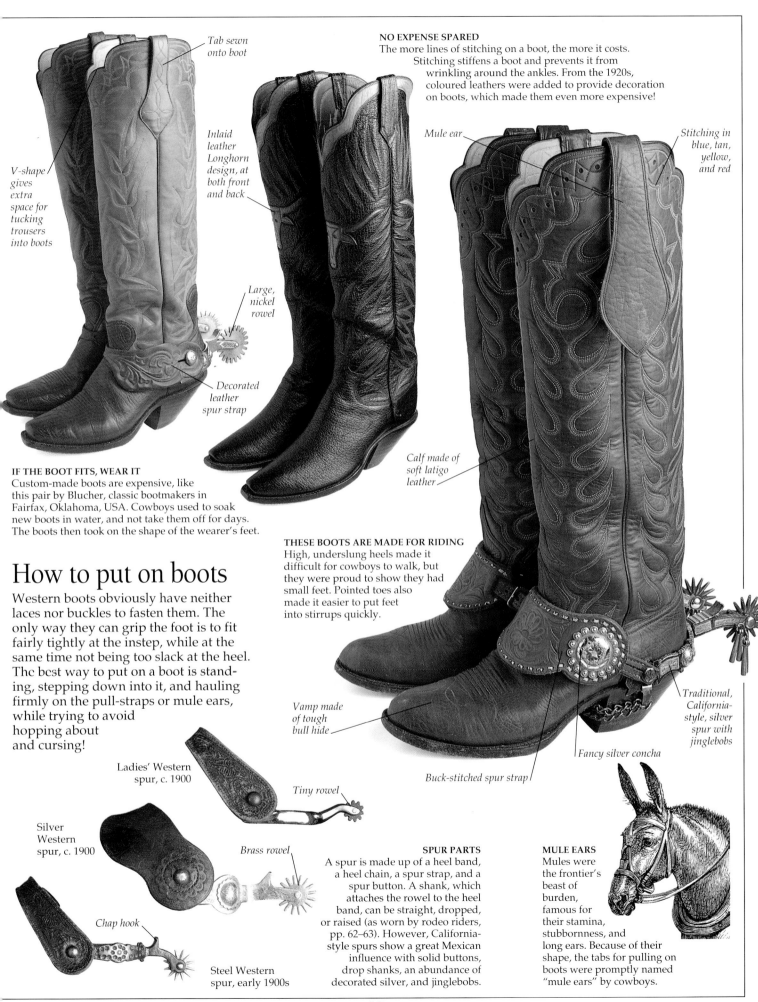

Tab sewn onto boot

V-shape gives extra space for tucking trousers into boots

Inlaid leather Longhorn design, at both front and back

Large, nickel rowel

Decorated leather spur strap

NO EXPENSE SPARED
The more lines of stitching on a boot, the more it costs. Stitching stiffens a boot and prevents it from wrinkling around the ankles. From the 1920s, coloured leathers were added to provide decoration on boots, which made them even more expensive!

Mule ear

Stitching in blue, tan, yellow, and red

Calf made of soft latigo leather

IF THE BOOT FITS, WEAR IT
Custom-made boots are expensive, like this pair by Blucher, classic bootmakers in Fairfax, Oklahoma, USA. Cowboys used to soak new boots in water, and not take them off for days. The boots then took on the shape of the wearer's feet.

THESE BOOTS ARE MADE FOR RIDING
High, underslung heels made it difficult for cowboys to walk, but they were proud to show they had small feet. Pointed toes also made it easier to put feet into stirrups quickly.

How to put on boots

Western boots obviously have neither laces nor buckles to fasten them. The only way they can grip the foot is to fit fairly tightly at the instep, while at the same time not being too slack at the heel. The best way to put on a boot is standing, stepping down into it, and hauling firmly on the pull-straps or mule ears, while trying to avoid hopping about and cursing!

Vamp made of tough bull hide

Traditional, California-style, silver spur with jinglebobs

Fancy silver concha

Buck-stitched spur strap

Ladies' Western spur, c. 1900

Tiny rowel

Silver Western spur, c. 1900

Brass rowel

Chap hook

Steel Western spur, early 1900s

SPUR PARTS
A spur is made up of a heel band, a heel chain, a spur strap, and a spur button. A shank, which attaches the rowel to the heel band, can be straight, dropped, or raised (as worn by rodeo riders, pp. 62–63). However, California-style spurs show a great Mexican influence with solid buttons, drop shanks, an abundance of decorated silver, and jinglebobs.

MULE EARS
Mules were the frontier's beast of burden, famous for their stamina, stubbornness, and long ears. Because of their shape, the tabs for pulling on boots were promptly named "mule ears" by cowboys.

Chaps in "chaps"

RIDING HARD THROUGH SPIKY BRUSH could rip a horseman's pants and legs! Mexican *vaqueros* (pp. 8–11) taught cowboys to protect themselves from the *chaparro prieto* (thornbrush) by wearing leather *chaparejos* (shortened to "chaps", pronounced "shaps"). Different styles emerged. Mexican *armitas* looked like a long, split apron, ending below the knee; "shotguns" and "batwings" were both ankle length and took their nicknames from their shapes. On colder northern ranges, chaps were made of Angora goat skin, nicknamed "woollies". Chaps also kept off rain, saved the rider from cattle horns and horse bites, and chafed knees when riding.

Back views of cowboys wearing *armitas* (left) and batwings (right)

Montana peak-style with distinctive dents

Fleece-lined waistcoat

Rawhide braiding on crown of Stetson

Denim bib-style shirt

SHOTGUN-STYLE CHAPS
This modern 1980s' cowboy is sporting shotgun chaps, which were made in California – the leather has been oiled to ensure that the chaps are waterproof. His shield-fronted, or "bib", shirt suggests he may be a fan of John Wayne, who wore them in many of his movies, although old-time cowboys would not have been likely to do so. This cowboy is enjoying his hobby of whittling a toy horse from a piece of wood.

Shotgun chaps with fringing down leg to keep the rain off

WINTER WOOLLIES
This 1880s' cowboy from Wyoming or Montana is dressed for the winter cold. His woollies are made from soft, curly, heavy buffalo hide and his linen bib shirt is expensive because it has been imported from the East. His Colt Lightning slide-action rifle can be fired very rapidly, but it needs constant cleaning and oiling, especially in winter, to prevent it jamming.

Woollie chaps

American quarter used as concha

ROMANTIC COWBOY
In this 1910 picture, a cowboy is wearing Angora goat chaps ("woollies"). By this date, the romantic image of the cowboy was hugely popular through the paintings of artists like Frederic Remington (1861–1909) and Charles Russell (1864–1926).

THREE KINDS OF CHAPS
These cowboys are wearing different kinds of chaps, which show how little the cowboys' clothing has changed since the 1860s. The lefthand cowboy is wearing heavy leather chaps from Canada in the 1970s. His shirt is cotton, not wool, and he is wearing a "wild rag" (bandana). The centre cowboy has on 1920s' leather cuffs and *armitas* with a built-in waistband and open pockets on the thighs. He is holding a lariat (from the Spanish *la riata*). The righthand cowboy is wearing custom-made, batwing-style, heavy leather parade chaps, with scalloped edging. He is holding a hackamore (from the Spanish *jaquima*) headstall, or bridle, used for training horses up to five years old.

Buckle fastening on outside of leg

Brand mark on chaps

18-m (60-ft) long lariat made from 4 strands of rawhide

Horsehair mecate, forming joined reins and lead rope

Braided rawhide bosal, or noseband

Fringe on outside leg only

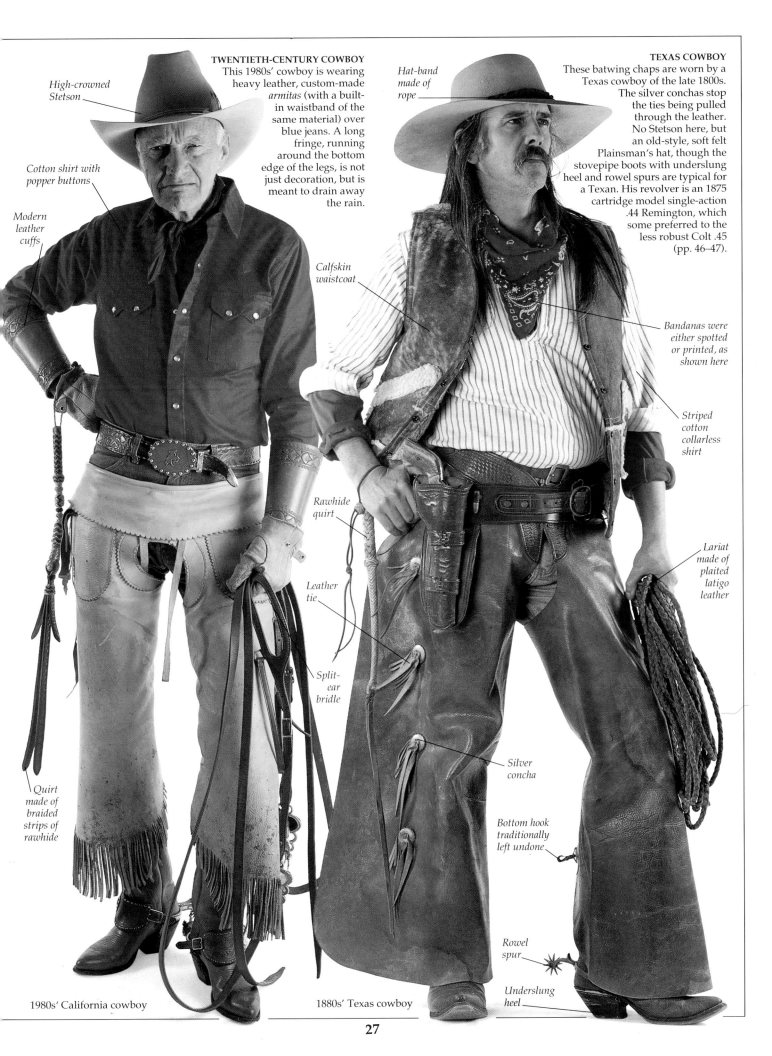

TWENTIETH-CENTURY COWBOY
This 1980s' cowboy is wearing heavy leather, custom-made *armitas* (with a built-in waistband of the same material) over blue jeans. A long fringe, running around the bottom edge of the legs, is not just decoration, but is meant to drain away the rain.

TEXAS COWBOY
These batwing chaps are worn by a Texas cowboy of the late 1800s. The silver conchas stop the ties being pulled through the leather. No Stetson here, but an old-style, soft felt Plainsman's hat, though the stovepipe boots with underslung heel and rowel spurs are typical for a Texan. His revolver is an 1875 cartridge model single-action .44 Remington, which some preferred to the less robust Colt .45 (pp. 46–47).

High-crowned Stetson

Cotton shirt with popper buttons

Modern leather cuffs

Hat-band made of rope

Calfskin waistcoat

Bandanas were either spotted or printed, as shown here

Striped cotton collarless shirt

Rawhide quirt

Leather tie

Split-ear bridle

Lariat made of plaited latigo leather

Silver concha

Quirt made of braided strips of rawhide

Bottom hook traditionally left undone

Rowel spur

Underslung heel

1980s' California cowboy

1880s' Texas cowboy

27

Life on a ranch

OUT ON THE GREAT GRASSLANDS, ranches had to be self-sufficient for long periods. In the late 1800s, American ranchers on the northern ranges might stock up with foodstuffs and equipment for a year at a time. In Australia's outback (pp. 56–57), immense distances separated cattle stations and settlements, enforcing real isolation. Families were dependent on painfully slow camel and bullock trains for mail and supplies. The Flying Doctor service since 1928, School of the Air (learning by radio) since 1951, and modern roads have been important improvements in Australia. Ranches and cattle stations needed a water supply close by. Buildings, usually made of timber, were designed to adapt to changing needs and to meet the demands of the climate.

DON'T FENCE ME IN
Barbed wire, invented in 1874, was used by homesteaders in the USA to protect their crops, and also by ranchers, especially after 1885–1886, to fence off good pasture and water (pp. 18–19). Cowboys really hated the restriction it brought and even more the new job of mending it.

WASTE NOT, WANT NOT
The horns and hide of cattle were made into a great variety of items – even household furniture, as shown by this chair from Kansas City, USA.

Cowhide seat

Leg made from a Longhorn's horn

Cross protects gardian in his home away from home

HOME AND AWAY
When work with his livestock took a Camargue *gardian* far from his home (pp. 52–53), he would find shelter in a *cabane*, rather like an American cowboy's line camp (a small, log cabin for overnight stays when away from ranch headquarters).

Brick chimney for stove used for both heating and cooking

Painted timber ranchhouse

Hitching rail for tying up horses

Bunkhouse made of logs

Shelf for holding a cowboy's shaving equipment

Chimney pipe to get rid of smoke from stove

"Dog trot"

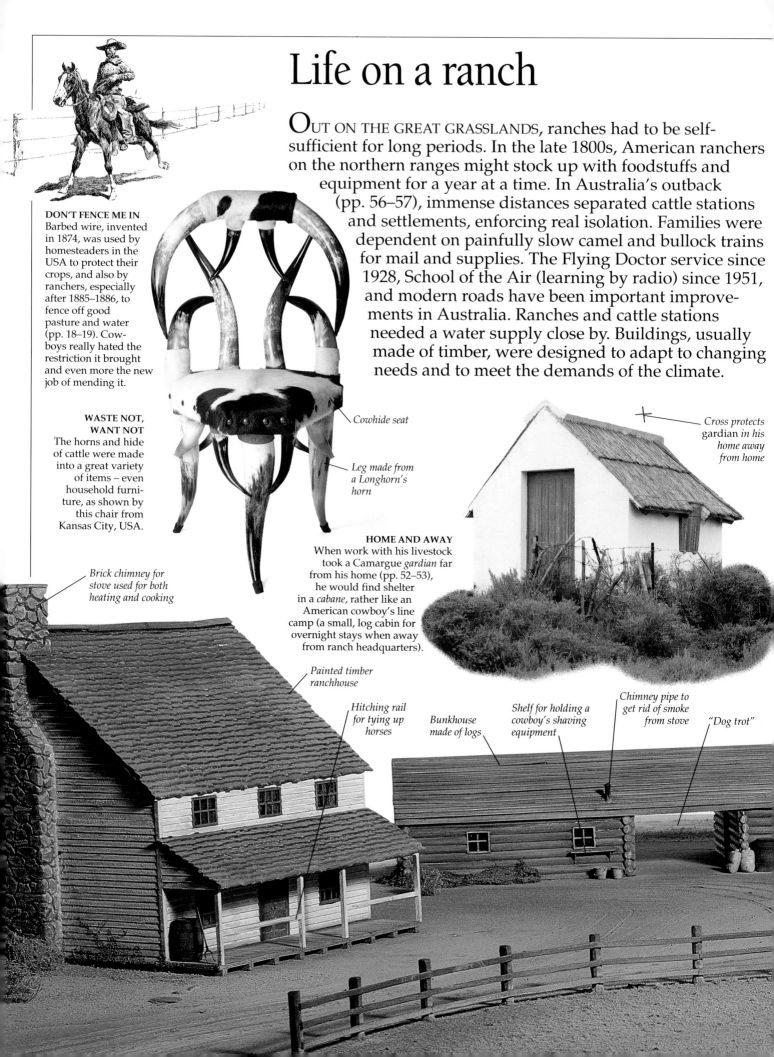

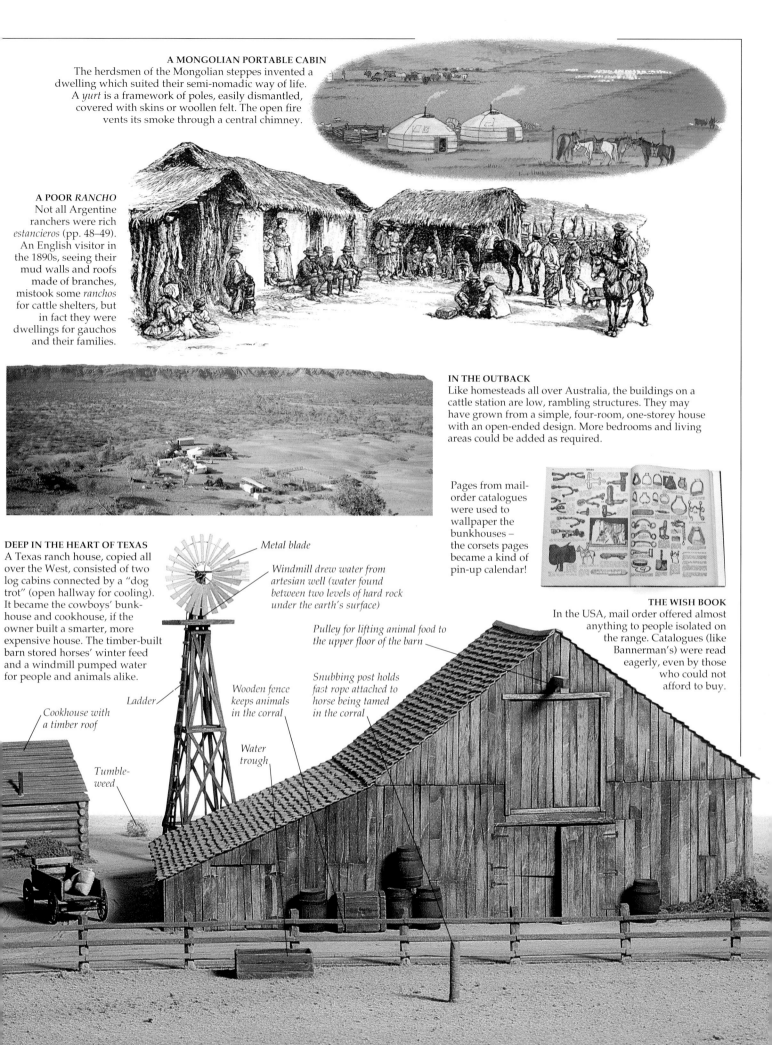

A MONGOLIAN PORTABLE CABIN

The herdsmen of the Mongolian steppes invented a dwelling which suited their semi-nomadic way of life. A *yurt* is a framework of poles, easily dismantled, covered with skins or woollen felt. The open fire vents its smoke through a central chimney.

A POOR *RANCHO*

Not all Argentine ranchers were rich *estancieros* (pp. 48–49). An English visitor in the 1890s, seeing their mud walls and roofs made of branches, mistook some *ranchos* for cattle shelters, but in fact they were dwellings for gauchos and their families.

IN THE OUTBACK

Like homesteads all over Australia, the buildings on a cattle station are low, rambling structures. They may have grown from a simple, four-room, one-storey house with an open-ended design. More bedrooms and living areas could be added as required.

Pages from mail-order catalogues were used to wallpaper the bunkhouses – the corsets pages became a kind of pin-up calendar!

THE WISH BOOK

In the USA, mail order offered almost anything to people isolated on the range. Catalogues (like Bannerman's) were read eagerly, even by those who could not afford to buy.

DEEP IN THE HEART OF TEXAS

A Texas ranch house, copied all over the West, consisted of two log cabins connected by a "dog trot" (open hallway for cooling). It became the cowboys' bunk-house and cookhouse, if the owner built a smarter, more expensive house. The timber-built barn stored horses' winter feed and a windmill pumped water for people and animals alike.

Metal blade

Windmill drew water from artesian well (water found between two levels of hard rock under the earth's surface)

Pulley for lifting animal food to the upper floor of the barn

Snubbing post holds fast rope attached to horse being tamed in the corral

Wooden fence keeps animals in the corral

Ladder

Cookhouse with a timber roof

Tumble-weed

Water trough

Cattle and branding

PEOPLE HAVE REARED CATTLE for thousands of years, but it was the population explosion of the 19th century in Europe and America which turned cattle raising into an industry. Demand for cheap meat encouraged ranching to spread across the world's great grasslands, so that it became an important enterprise in the USA, Canada, Brazil, Argentina, and Australia. No cattle existed in any of these countries before European settlers brought them. European cattle were originally hardy, but lean. From the 1770s, however, a breeding revolution in Britain produced new, heavy beef strains like the Hereford, Shorthorn, and Aberdeen Angus. From the 1870s, these were increasingly exported to replace or cross-breed with the old European Longhorns in the New World. In Spain and in the Camargue in southern France, bulls are still bred solely for fighting.

WHERE THE BUFFALO ROAM
Up to the 1860s, millions of buffalo roamed the North American plains. They were ruthlessly slaughtered for their meat and skins by hunters like Buffalo Bill Cody (1846–1917). At a low point in their breeding cycle, buffalo nearly became extinct.

SUCCESS STORY
Herefords, with their distinctive red and white colouring, are considered to be the most successful of the beef breeds and are renowned for their hardiness, early maturity, and swift, efficient conversion of grass into meat. In the American West, they were imported from Britain into the northern ranges in the early 1880s and, cross-bred with local cattle, they eventually replaced Longhorns in Wyoming and Montana. With their ability to thrive anywhere, there are now more than five million pedigree Herefords in over 50 countries.

Typical white head of Hereford

TEXAS LONGHORNS
Descendants of Spanish cattle imported in the 1520s, Longhorns spread from Mexico into the American West. Always half-wild, they were fierce and bad tempered. Though poor quality beef – mostly muscle – they were very hardy and could survive on the sparse grass of the dry plains.

As well as its original brand, a steer had a road (trail) brand added behind its left ear at the start of a cattle drive north from Texas

Two branding irons from North America

MAKING A MARK
Branding was the easiest means for a rancher to identify the ownership of cattle roaming the open range. Marks, usually simple shapes or letters, or combinations such as Bar T (– **T**) or Circle B (**O B**), were burnt through the hair into the surface of the animal's hide with red hot irons. Cowmen claimed this was relatively pain-free – cows probably thought otherwise!

This magnificent, 6-year-old, prize-winning, pedigree Hereford bull, named "Ironside", weighs 1,400 kg (3,100 lb) and stands 1.7 m (5 ft 6 in) at the flank.

DISPUTING A BRAND
Rustlers, or cattle thieves, tried various dodges to claim cattle. They might brand over an existing mark, or use a "running iron" (like a big iron poker) to change a brand. For example, Bar C would look like "–C" and could be changed easily to Lazy T Circle "⊦O" (where the "T" appears to be on its side). Originally, wandering "mavericks" (calves which had left their mothers) could be branded by whoever found them, but ranchers soon tried to stop this.

FRENCH MARKS
The fierce black bulls of the French Camargue are raised by local ranchers solely for the exciting and dangerous sport of the *course à la cocarde* (pp. 54–55). Each rancher separates the yearlings annually at the *ferrade*, or branding, and stamps them with their owner's mark – just as in the American West.

Branding irons from the French Camargue are used for both horses and bulls

BRITISH BLACK BULL
The Aberdeen Angus was originally bred, as its name indicates, in Aberdeenshire in Scotland. This is a naturally hornless breed which matures quickly (so it is ready for market early). It yields a high proportion of high quality meat – some say it makes the best steaks. The breed was first introduced into the USA in 1873.

"Volvo", a 20-month-old pure-bred Aberdeen Angus bull by a Canadian sire

BY A SHORT HORN
Shorthorns (shown in this 1890s' engraving) were first bred in the county of Durham in England. They were the most popular of the new breeds until replaced by the Hereford. Shorthorns were exported to Australia, Argentina, and the USA. The first Shorthorn register in the USA was set up in 1846 and in Canada in 1867. Shorthorns were brought to the West's northern ranges during the 1870s.

Herefords usually have their horns removed (polling) when calves

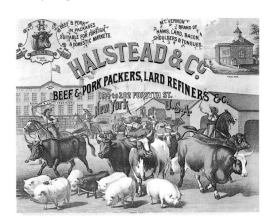

"Emma" is a 6-month-old Hereford calf, sired by "Ironside"

CANNED MEAT
Most big American cities had meatpackers, firms preserving and packaging meat for transporting to market. Those buying Western beef were centred in cities like St. Louis, Kansas City, and above all Chicago. This New York company's absurd 1880s' advertisement shows Mexican *vaqueros* on a New York dock.

Cutting cattle out of a herd

FAST STOP
Stopping quickly from a gallop needs powerful braking! The "fast stop" is used both in cutting out and when roping (pp. 34–35). The horse brings the back legs forward, throws its weight back, braces its front legs, and skids to a stop. In reining pattern classes at Western riding shows (above), the horse aims to complete a "sliding halt" within 7.5 to 9 m (25–30 ft).

SEPARATING A SINGLE ANIMAL from a whole herd of uneasy cattle, resentful of interference, was a routine task at the round-up. Nevertheless, it took skill and a real partnership between horse and rider to deal with a dodging, panicky cow – the process was called "cutting out". It was necessary in order to remove strange cattle which had accidentally been gathered up, but mostly to brand yearlings and calves (pp. 30–31). Top-class cutting horses were much valued and mustangs seemed to have instinctive "cow sense". With a little training, the most alert and intelligent horse could be pointed at the animal to be caught and would follow it through every twist and turn with hardly any use of the reins. One Western story tells of a cutting horse that brought a jackrabbit out of a herd!

1 SELECTING THE CALF
Horse and rider must begin cutting out quietly, so as not to alarm the herd, or indeed the animal selected, until as late as possible. The rider keeps a slack rein and the horse has its eyes fixed on the target.

2 SEPARATING THE CALF
Once the target starts to run, a frantic dashing and dodging competition between horse and calf begins. The horse will try to keep itself between the calf and the herd, to force the calf into the open and towards the branding fire.

Both rider and horse maintain eye contact with the calf during cutting

Quarter Horse, "Dust My Tucker", is an excellent cutting horse – a 7-year-old female, 15.1 hands high (1.9 m, 5 ft 1 in)

Horse swings in one direction, but is poised to turn abruptly in the opposite direction if necessary

"CUTTIN' CRITTER"

Old-time cowboys do not seem to have given their horses much training, relying on those which showed natural intelligence and ability to learn cutting out by doing it. Today, horses can be trained by a "cuttin' critter" – a motorized plastic calf on rails which is moved quickly and changes direction abruptly.

MEXICAN-STYLE DRIVE

Some Spanish-American *vaqueros* (pp. 10–11) used brutal forms of training for their horses. To teach them obedience to the reins, horses would be blindfolded and run full tilt at a wall! These modern Mexican cowboys are chivvying along some zebu cattle (pp. 50–51).

Horse assumes a threatening expression, with its ears flattened to intimidate the calf

GET OUT OF THAT

Western story magazines flourished after 1910 and their cover illustrations were often by well-known action artists. In search of excitement this artist has got his cowboy in serious difficulties. Hopefully, his horse will know what to do – because the rider obviously does not!

WEST
1/-   LATE DECEMBER

JAMES STEVENS
GEORGE C FRANKLIN

SKEETER BILL FINDS A GUN
BY W C TUTTLE

Calf is mix of Hereford and Aberdeen Angus breeds

Loose reins allow horse to follow its instinct with no instruction from the rider

Rider's feet, as well as legs and body, give clear signals to horse when it is working

3 TURNING THE CALF

Once in the open the target animal will make desperate attempts to get back to the herd – wheeling, baulking, and ducking behind the horse. The best cutting horses can stop short from a gallop and immediately sprint off in a new direction. Riders must stay in balance with their horses, or they will be thrown.

WHICH WAY NEXT?

This is how the target appears to the cutting horse – small, stubborn, and agile. This calf is a Hereford-Aberdeen Angus cross, but no less trouble for that.

Continued on next page

THE FINE ART OF ROPING
Roping was a skill so impressive that it became entertainment. Cowboys in Buffalo Bill's Wild West show (pp. 60–61) demonstrated roping tricks and, after 1900, roping acts in vaudeville (theatrical) shows became popular. For many years, the much loved entertainer Will Rogers (1870–1935) combined trick roping with comedy in his stage act.

South American lariat made of rawhide

Early sisal rope made of plaited hemp (c. 1890s)

Modern Western rope made of hemp

EITHER HIDE OR HAIR – OR GRASS
Originally, cowboys copied Mexican *vaqueros'* plaited rawhide lariats, widely used throughout Spanish America. Then they adopted the plaited, grass rope, or one made from sisal (the stiff fibres of the Mexican agave plant). Modern ropes are made from nylon, or a mixture of man-made fibres and grass.

The cowboy holds the "piggin' string" between his teeth in a rodeo event

Hondo, or eyelet

Catch rope is thrown around calf's head in a rodeo event

TAKING AIM
For a small calf, a working cowboy would use a heel catch, casting sideways to slip the rope under the animal's hind legs. It could then be dragged conveniently to the branding fire.

CAUGHT SHORT
Mexican *vaqueros* taught American cowboys their trade (pp. 10–11). It was they who first perfected skills with the lariat (*la reata*) and developed roping techniques for dealing with range cattle and horses.

In a rodeo event, calf is roped around its head – its feet are tied with a "piggin' string" made from fine rope

Horse wears protective boots on its legs during a rodeo event

LOOP THE LOOP
Old-time Mongolian herdsmen did not develop a rope for capturing wild horses. Instead they invented an ingenious long pole with a noose at the end to slip over the horse's head. Manipulating pole and noose must have required as much skill as using a lariat.

Using a lariat

About 12 m (40 ft) long, one end of the lariat, or rope, is slipped through an eyelet (the honda) to make a large loop. A right-handed cowboy holds the loop (with the honda part way down) and part of the rope in his right hand, while the rest of the rope is coiled in his left hand. Whirling it only a couple of times to gain momentum, the cowboy flings the loop at the target. The stiff rope fibre keeps the loop flat and open until jerked tight.

EL RODEO STAR
Roping became one of the basic events in rodeo riding – as shown in this 1924 sketch by artist Charles Simpson.

IT TAKES TWO
For roping cattle, a cowboy needs only two basic throws. A "head" catch is thrown around the horns (around the neck might strangle the beast), while a "heel" catch is aimed at the back legs to trip it.

Because a dally might slip and the cow escape, the rope may be tied to the horn in advance

Rear of saddle tips up as pressure is applied to the horn by the roped steer or calf

Flank cinch tightens as dallied rope is pulled tight by roped animal – the horse must work to keep rope taut when cowboy dismounts

A TIME TO DALLY
As a cow is roped, the cowboy "dallies" (from the Spanish *dar la vuelta* for give a turn), or turns, his rope around the saddle horn. Alternatively, he can tie the rope to the horn in a figure of eight knot (left). The horse digs in or backs up to keep the rope taut, the saddle taking the strain. If a cowboy is a fraction late taking a dally and his hand is caught between rope and horn, the shock of the cow's weight on the rope might cut off his fingers.

Home on the range

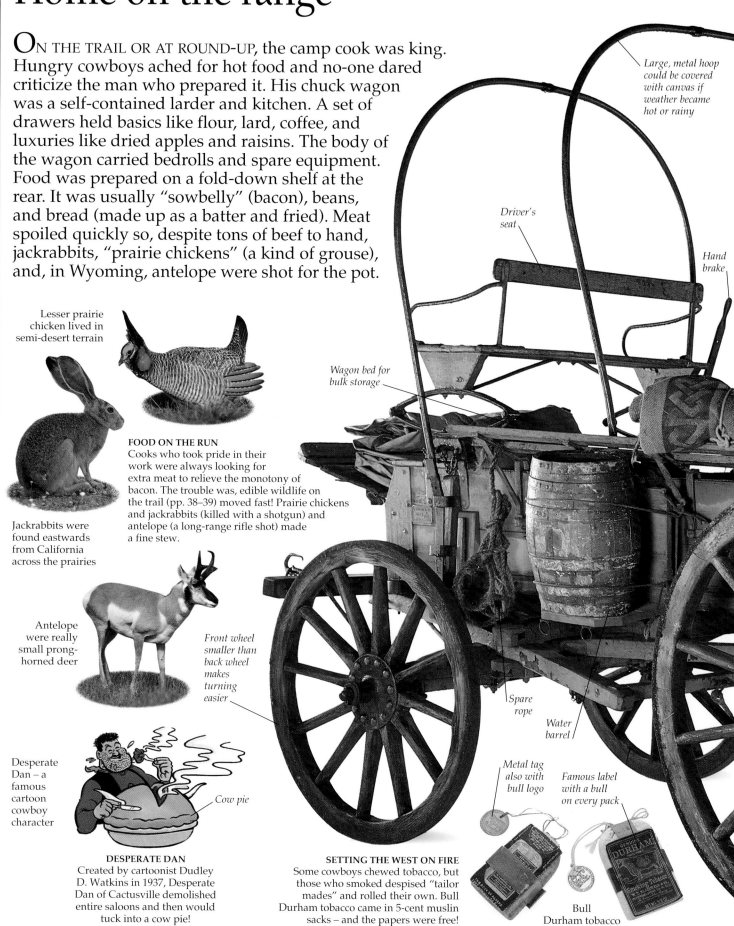

On THE TRAIL OR AT ROUND-UP, the camp cook was king. Hungry cowboys ached for hot food and no-one dared criticize the man who prepared it. His chuck wagon was a self-contained larder and kitchen. A set of drawers held basics like flour, lard, coffee, and luxuries like dried apples and raisins. The body of the wagon carried bedrolls and spare equipment. Food was prepared on a fold-down shelf at the rear. It was usually "sowbelly" (bacon), beans, and bread (made up as a batter and fried). Meat spoiled quickly so, despite tons of beef to hand, jackrabbits, "prairie chickens" (a kind of grouse), and, in Wyoming, antelope were shot for the pot.

Large, metal hoop could be covered with canvas if weather became hot or rainy

Driver's seat

Hand brake

Lesser prairie chicken lived in semi-desert terrain

Wagon bed for bulk storage

FOOD ON THE RUN
Cooks who took pride in their work were always looking for extra meat to relieve the monotony of bacon. The trouble was, edible wildlife on the trail (pp. 38–39) moved fast! Prairie chickens and jackrabbits (killed with a shotgun) and antelope (a long-range rifle shot) made a fine stew.

Jackrabbits were found eastwards from California across the prairies

Antelope were really small prong-horned deer

Front wheel smaller than back wheel makes turning easier

Spare rope

Water barrel

Cow pie

Desperate Dan – a famous cartoon cowboy character

Metal tag also with bull logo

Famous label with a bull on every pack

DESPERATE DAN
Created by cartoonist Dudley D. Watkins in 1937, Desperate Dan of Cactusville demolished entire saloons and then would tuck into a cow pie!

SETTING THE WEST ON FIRE
Some cowboys chewed tobacco, but those who smoked despised "tailor mades" and rolled their own. Bull Durham tobacco came in 5-cent muslin sacks – and the papers were free!

Bull Durham tobacco

CHUCK WAGON SPECIAL
The first design for a chuck wagon was made by cattleman Charles Goodnight in 1866, when he adapted an old army wagon. He added four pieces of equipment – a barrel holding two days' supply of water, a heavy tool box, hoops for a protective canvas, and, most important of all, a chuck box.

Chuck box (set of drawers) containing cook's basic necessities – flour, coffee, beans, sugar, even grain for the wagon team

Metal lantern, with handle

Skillet

Coffee cup

Bedroll

CHOW'S UP!
Cowboy meals were no picnic! The food was boring and unhealthy and cooks were often "stove-up" (injured) former cowboys with no skills. Hygiene was non-existent – cups and plates were thrown into the "wreck pan" and just scoured with sand if water was not plentiful. It is hardly surprising that cowboys, when they got to town (pp. 42–43), spent their money on eggs and steaks, as well as liquor.

Tools, such as a shovel, axe, and branding irons were stored in a tool box (under chuck box)

Dried fruit

Useful extra hook

Metal plate

Brake for rear wheel

"Wreck pan"

Large pot for cooking stews over an open campfire

Support for hinged lid of chuck box swings down to form work table for the cook

Apron made from old canvas bag

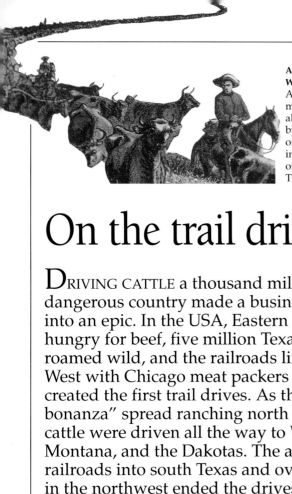

On the trail drive

DRIVING CATTLE a thousand miles across dangerous country made a business venture into an epic. In the USA, Eastern cities were hungry for beef, five million Texas cattle roamed wild, and the railroads linked the West with Chicago meat packers – all this created the first trail drives. As the "beef bonanza" spread ranching north in 1880–1881, cattle were driven all the way to Wyoming, Montana, and the Dakotas. The advance of railroads into south Texas and overstocking in the northwest ended the drives in the early 1880s. In Australia, overlanders seeking new pastures pioneered stock routes (trails) through uncharted country sometimes defended by hostile Aboriginals. In 1883, 8,000 cattle were driven a record 4,000 km (2,500 miles)!

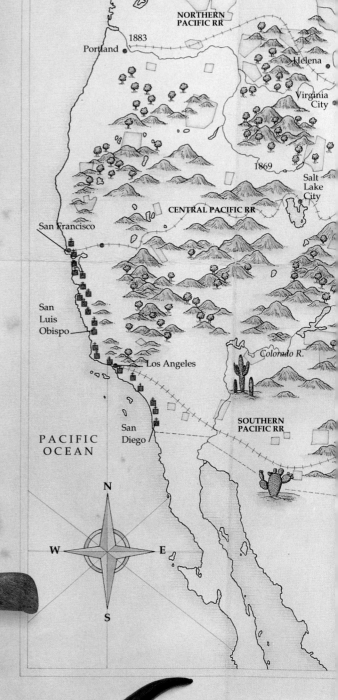

Two bowie-style knives, c. 1900

Bone handle

Wooden handle

Blood groove in steel blade

DANGEROUS KNIVES
Made popular by the Texan adventurer, Colonel James Bowie (1799–1836), the bowie (pronounced *boowie*) knife was a formidable weapon. Most cowboys carried an all-purpose knife, but the bowie knife was intended for fighting, though it was also used by hunters.

Set of Longhorn's horns measuring 1.5 m (5 ft) from tip to tip

HOW LONG ARE A LONGHORN'S HORNS?
Texas cattle indeed had very long horns – a spread of 1.5 m (5 ft) was common! Descendants of Iberian cattle brought by the Spaniards (pp. 30–31), they had been left to breed untended during the American Civil War (1861–1865). Cowboys knew that Longhorns were truly wild beasts – fierce, mean-tempered, and dangerous – and that a herd was trouble waiting to happen (pp. 40–41).

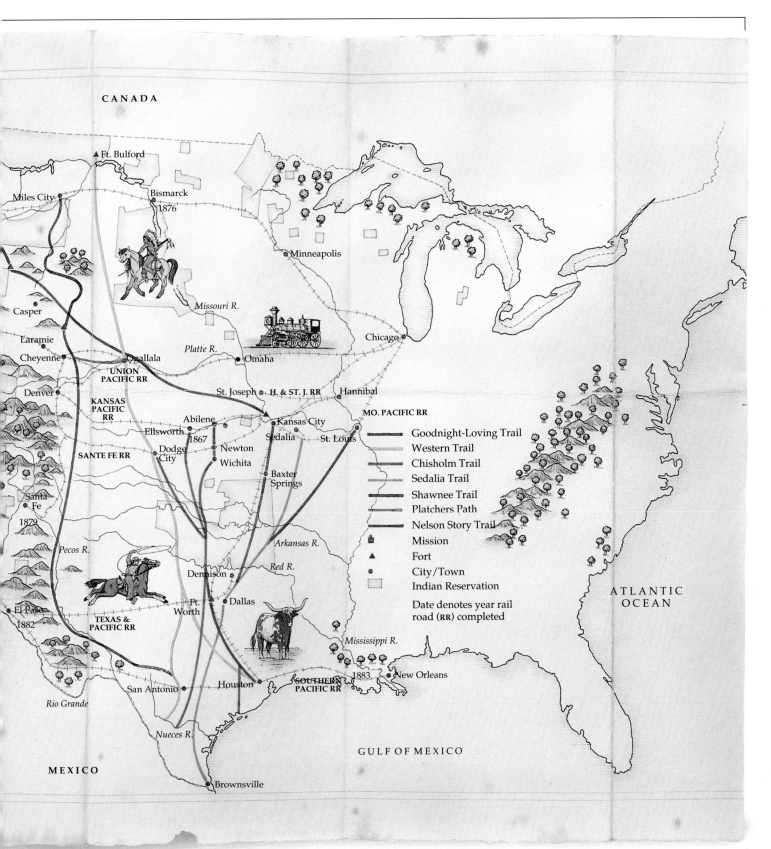

CANADA

Ft. Bulford

Miles City

Bismarck
1876

Minneapolis

Missouri R.

Casper

Chicago

Laramie

Cheyenne

Ogallala
UNION
PACIFIC RR

Platte R.
Omaha

Denver

KANSAS
PACIFIC
RR

St. Joseph   H. & ST. J. RR   Hannibal

Abilene
Ellsworth

Kansas City

MO. PACIFIC RR

SANTE FE RR

Dodge
City

1867

Newton
Wichita

Sedalia
St. Louis

Goodnight-Loving Trail
Western Trail
Chisholm Trail
Sedalia Trail
Shawnee Trail
Platchers Path
Nelson Story Trail

Santa
Fe
1879

Baxter
Springs

Mission
Fort
City/Town
Indian Reservation

Pecos R.

Arkansas R.

Red R.

Dennison

Date denotes year rail
road (RR) completed

El Paso
1882

TEXAS &
PACIFIC RR

Ft.
Worth

Dallas

ATLANTIC
OCEAN

Mississippi R.

Rio Grande

Houston

SOUTHERN
PACIFIC RR

1883   New Orleans

San Antonio

Nueces R.

GULF OF MEXICO

MEXICO

Brownsville

WET WEATHER
Trailing a herd in
a northwest
winter was
miserable
work! Oilskin
slickers were
the only protection
against rain and snow.

NORTHWARD HO!
Jesse Chisholm
(1806–1868) laid out
a supply route from
Texas to Kansas
during the
Civil War – it
later became a
trail for herds
heading to
Abilene.

EPIC JOURNEYS
Cattle trails linked ranges with railroads. In 1866
fear of Texas fever infecting local cattle closed the
Missouri border and the trails which led there.
The alternative Chisholm Trail carried two million
cattle up to the Kansas railheads between 1867 and
1871. In the 1870s, the Western Trail ran directly
to Dodge City. Named after two ranchers, the
Goodnight-Loving Trail was laid out in 1866 to
supply Colorado mining camps, but was soon used
to stock the ranges of Wyoming and Montana.

Continued on next page

Dangers on the trail

A trail drive was not fun – it was hours of stupefying boredom interspersed with moments of acute danger. Cowboys rarely saw hostile Indians. Mostly they rode the flanks of a herd to stop cows wandering off, while the "drag rider" at the rear, choking on dust, chivvied stragglers. The main worry was finding water at the end of the day. But range cattle were easily alarmed, "ornery" (mean-tempered), and not very smart. At a river crossing they might not only drown themselves but in panic drown a cowboy too. The biggest threat was a stampede, where a second's mistake in a sea of tossing horns and pounding hooves was a death sentence.

Starr .44 revolver (1858) was one of the first double-action, or self-cocking, models

Nipple

Soft cap

Walnut grip

Colt model 1851 Navy .36 revolver

Tin holding percussion caps

Flask containing gunpowder

STAMPEDE!
Cattle were mindlessly nervous. A herd might be spooked by any unexpected sight, a sudden noise, or unusual scent – certainly lightning would terrorize them! The animals would then, without warning, burst into a stampede, running for miles. The cowboys' only hope was to race to the head of the herd and, by firing pistols, waving hats, and yelling, frighten the leaders into turning until the whole herd began to "mill", or circle, aimlessly.

FOOD ON THE HOOF
Grizzly bears saw horses and cattle as food. Ferocious, 2.4 m (8 ft) in height and weighing up to 365 kg (800 lb), grizzlies were an infrequent, but serious, hazard. These teeth belonged to a grizzly shot in British Columbia, Canada, after killing livestock. The rifle cartridge shows how big these teeth were.

PACKING A PISTOL
Cowboys mostly used their revolvers to deal with the dangers on the trail. They might need to shoot a fatally injured horse, a maddened steer, or a rattlesnake. Pistols were fired in the air to turn a stampeding herd or give the traditional distress signal (three shots).

CRY WOLF
The American timber wolf was a serious problem to ranchers. Wolves were not a threat to people but after the buffalo had been wiped out (pp. 30–31), they preyed on calves and colts. They were killed by traps or poisoned with bait laced with strychnine.

NOT A CUDDLY TOY!
Brown bears ranged across America wherever the country was wild, mountainous, or forested. They were omnivores (eating animals and plants) and learned to add calves to their diet. Up to 1.8 m (6 ft) long and weighing from 90 to 250 kg (200–500 lb), they were dangerous if alarmed.

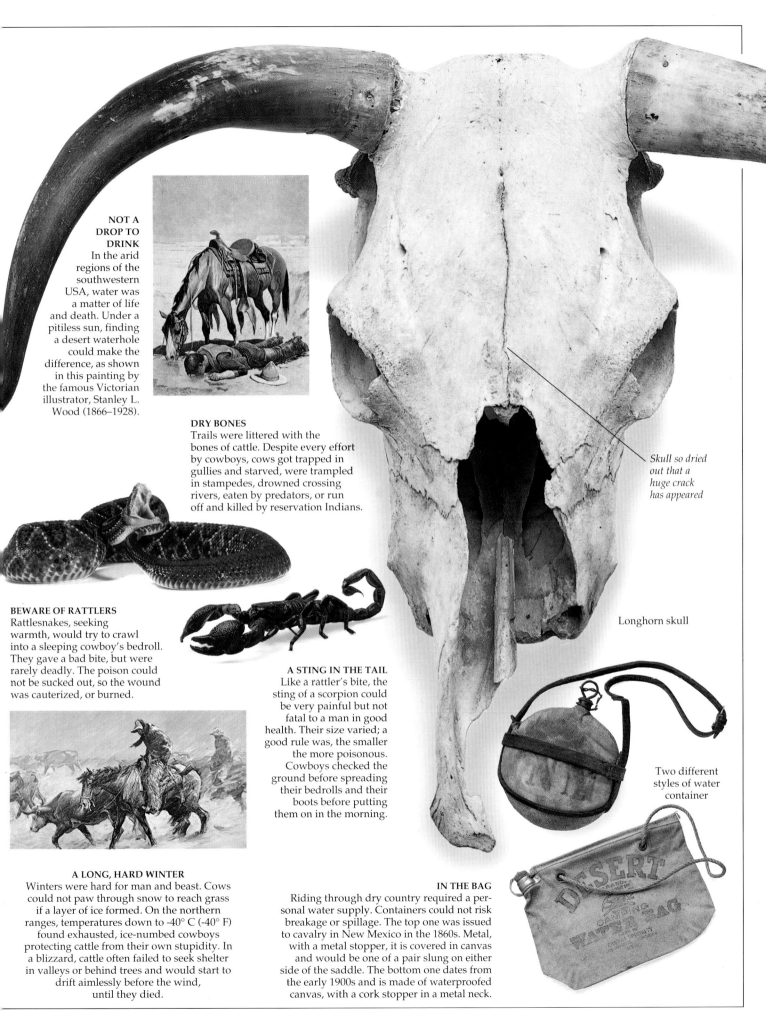

NOT A DROP TO DRINK
In the arid regions of the southwestern USA, water was a matter of life and death. Under a pitiless sun, finding a desert waterhole could make the difference, as shown in this painting by the famous Victorian illustrator, Stanley L. Wood (1866–1928).

DRY BONES
Trails were littered with the bones of cattle. Despite every effort by cowboys, cows got trapped in gullies and starved, were trampled in stampedes, drowned crossing rivers, eaten by predators, or run off and killed by reservation Indians.

BEWARE OF RATTLERS
Rattlesnakes, seeking warmth, would try to crawl into a sleeping cowboy's bedroll. They gave a bad bite, but were rarely deadly. The poison could not be sucked out, so the wound was cauterized, or burned.

A STING IN THE TAIL
Like a rattler's bite, the sting of a scorpion could be very painful but not fatal to a man in good health. Their size varied; a good rule was, the smaller the more poisonous. Cowboys checked the ground before spreading their bedrolls and their boots before putting them on in the morning.

A LONG, HARD WINTER
Winters were hard for man and beast. Cows could not paw through snow to reach grass if a layer of ice formed. On the northern ranges, temperatures down to -40° C (-40° F) found exhausted, ice-numbed cowboys protecting cattle from their own stupidity. In a blizzard, cattle often failed to seek shelter in valleys or behind trees and would start to drift aimlessly before the wind, until they died.

IN THE BAG
Riding through dry country required a personal water supply. Containers could not risk breakage or spillage. The top one was issued to cavalry in New Mexico in the 1860s. Metal, with a metal stopper, it is covered in canvas and would be one of a pair slung on either side of the saddle. The bottom one dates from the early 1900s and is made of waterproofed canvas, with a cork stopper in a metal neck.

Skull so dried out that a huge crack has appeared

Longhorn skull

Two different styles of water container

Law and order

SHOOTOUT
Street gunfights were not as usual as Westerns suggest. Remington's drawing may be based on the shootout between Luke Short and Jim Courtright at Fort Worth, Texas in 1887.

Sheriff's gaol keys

S TEELY-EYED LAWMEN, fast on the draw, kept the peace on Hollywood's frontier. In the real West things were usually less exciting. An elected county sheriff's main work included collecting local taxes as well as law enforcement. Town marshals, usually appointed by the city council, were expected to enforce health and safety regulations, collect licence fees, and serve warrants. Both jobs offered power and opportunity to make money, so there was keen competition. Only in cowtowns and mining communities, and there only while conditions required it, were law officers gunmen.

Marshal's badge made of silver (c. 1870)

Deputy's badge made of silver (1897)

DEPUTY LAWMAN
Shady characters as well as honest lawmen could become US Deputy Marshals. Wyatt Earp's brother Virgil (1843–1906) held this post in Arizona in 1879.

MARSHAL OF DEADWOOD
The Marshal of Deadwood, a mining town in Dakota Territory, had to deal with frequent stage robberies and the murder of Wild Bill Hickok (1837–1876).

"JAILBIRD"
The death penalty was unusual in the West. Prison, like the Yuma penitentiary in Arizona Territory, was the fate of many badmen. Here is an example of a 1900s' prison guard's brass badge.

Special agent's badge, made of nickel

Bank guard's badge, made of nickel

Rail road police badge, made of nickel

SPECIAL AGENTS
The powerful stage line and banking firm, Wells, Fargo, employed its own guards and company police. Its Special Agents were detectives, competent and tireless in tracking down those who preyed on it.

PAINTING THE TOWN RED
After three months or more on the trail (pp. 38–39), Texas cowboys quickly spent their hard-earned money in the cowtowns of Kansas on liquor, gambling, and women. Even in good humour they might shoot up the town and, if unchecked, they readily turned to serious violence. Strong law enforcement was demanded by respectable citizens. Wichita (above) had seven marshals from 1868 to 1871 – all ineffective until the firm rule of Michael Meager (1871–1874) brought order.

Pinkerton badge (1860)

TEXAS RANGERS FOREVER
First raised in 1835, the Texas Rangers were reformed in 1873 into a Frontier Battalion to deal with Indians and the Special Force for bandits and rustlers. Since 1935, the Rangers have been part of the Department of Public Safety.

THE PINKERTON AGENT
The Pinkerton Detective Agency was a formidable private organization. It was detested in the West for bombing the James family (pp. 44–45) home in 1875 and for breaking miners' strikes in the 1880s.

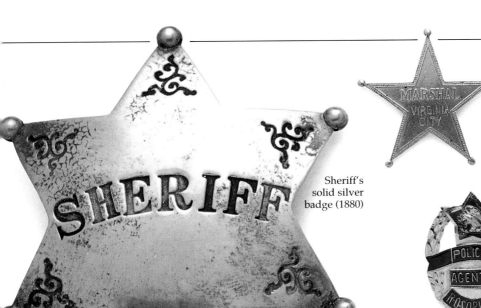

Sheriff's solid silver badge (1880)

A LAWLESS TOWN
Mark Twain (1835–1910) as a young journalist knew Virginia City, Nevada, as a "wide-open" mining town in the 1860s, when violence was commonplace.

Virginia City Marshal's badge (c. 1860–1880)

MEXICAN LAWMEN
Mexico's history in the 1800s had been very different from that of the USA. Outside the cities, order was kept by the detested *guardia rurales* (police cavalry). Towns, like Ensenada, had a regular police force.

Three Mexican badges (c. 1900), made of copper-plate (top right) and brass

"HIGH SHERIFF"
As elected officials, sheriffs had to be politicians and some used the office to get rich. Many delegated law enforcement to deputies but others, like Bat Masterson (1853–1921) in Ford County, Kansas from 1877 to 1879, hunted outlaws and fought Indians.

Reproduction of a U.S. Marshal's brass badge (c. 1900)

Indian Police badge (c. 1880s)

FEDERAL MARSHAL
Appointed directly by the President, usually as a political reward, Federal Marshals might be just local businessmen and some turned out to be crooks. Others, like Evett Nix of Oklahoma Territory in the 1890s, were dedicated lawmen and appointed deputies like the famous Heck Thomas.

THE INDIAN POLICE
Indian Police were first tried as an experiment in the middle 1870s on the San Carlos Apache reservation in Arizona. In 1878, Congress set up Indian Police at each reservation agency. Reformers hoped this would be one more way to break tribal customs and make Indians "Americans".

A collection of items belonging to Wyatt Earp (1848–1929)

The good guys?

Desperate city councils sometimes appointed gunmen to deal with gunmen, as Abilene hired Wild Bill Hickok in 1871. However, journalists at the time (and film-makers later) have made legends out of dubious figures who held the job of lawmen, notably Wyatt Earp – who was involved with gambling and prostitution.

A job in Dodge City Earp refused

LEGENDARY LAWMAN
Wyatt Earp held police posts in Wichita (1874) and Dodge City (1878). A feud with the Clantons in Tombstone, Arizona led to the famous gunfight at the O.K. Corral in October 1881. Later he tried gambling and prospecting and ended up hanging around film sets in Hollywood. His fame as a Galahad among lawmen was entirely invented by Stuart Lake's 1931 book *Frontier Marshal*.

$20 gold piece

Horn tobacco pouch made by Earp's father

Guns and gunslingers

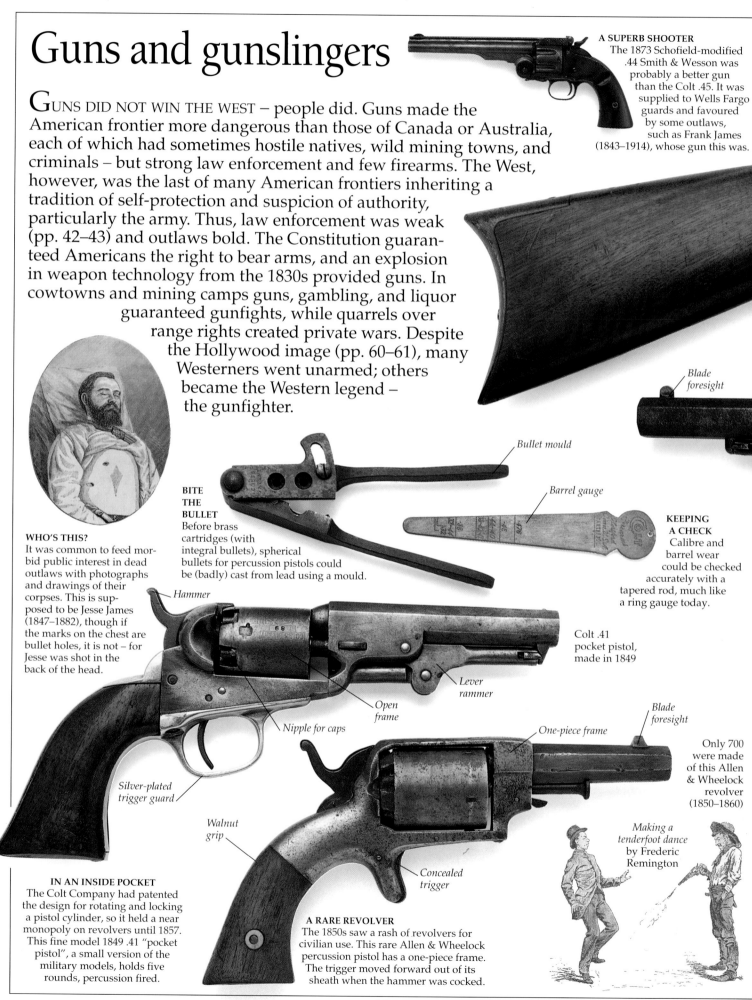

GUNS DID NOT WIN THE WEST – people did. Guns made the American frontier more dangerous than those of Canada or Australia, each of which had sometimes hostile natives, wild mining towns, and criminals – but strong law enforcement and few firearms. The West, however, was the last of many American frontiers inheriting a tradition of self-protection and suspicion of authority, particularly the army. Thus, law enforcement was weak (pp. 42–43) and outlaws bold. The Constitution guaranteed Americans the right to bear arms, and an explosion in weapon technology from the 1830s provided guns. In cowtowns and mining camps guns, gambling, and liquor guaranteed gunfights, while quarrels over range rights created private wars. Despite the Hollywood image (pp. 60–61), many Westerners went unarmed; others became the Western legend – the gunfighter.

A SUPERB SHOOTER
The 1873 Schofield-modified .44 Smith & Wesson was probably a better gun than the Colt .45. It was supplied to Wells Fargo guards and favoured by some outlaws, such as Frank James (1843–1914), whose gun this was.

Blade foresight

BITE THE BULLET
Before brass cartridges (with integral bullets), spherical bullets for percussion pistols could be (badly) cast from lead using a mould.

Bullet mould

Barrel gauge

KEEPING A CHECK
Calibre and barrel wear could be checked accurately with a tapered rod, much like a ring gauge today.

WHO'S THIS?
It was common to feed morbid public interest in dead outlaws with photographs and drawings of their corpses. This is supposed to be Jesse James (1847–1882), though if the marks on the chest are bullet holes, it is not – for Jesse was shot in the back of the head.

Hammer

Colt .41 pocket pistol, made in 1849

Lever rammer

Open frame

Nipple for caps

One-piece frame

Blade foresight

Only 700 were made of this Allen & Wheelock revolver (1850–1860)

Silver-plated trigger guard

Walnut grip

Concealed trigger

Making a tenderfoot dance by Frederic Remington

IN AN INSIDE POCKET
The Colt Company had patented the design for rotating and locking a pistol cylinder, so it held a near monopoly on revolvers until 1857. This fine model 1849 .41 "pocket pistol", a small version of the military models, holds five rounds, percussion fired.

A RARE REVOLVER
The 1850s saw a rash of revolvers for civilian use. This rare Allen & Wheelock percussion pistol has a one-piece frame. The trigger moved forward out of its sheath when the hammer was cocked.

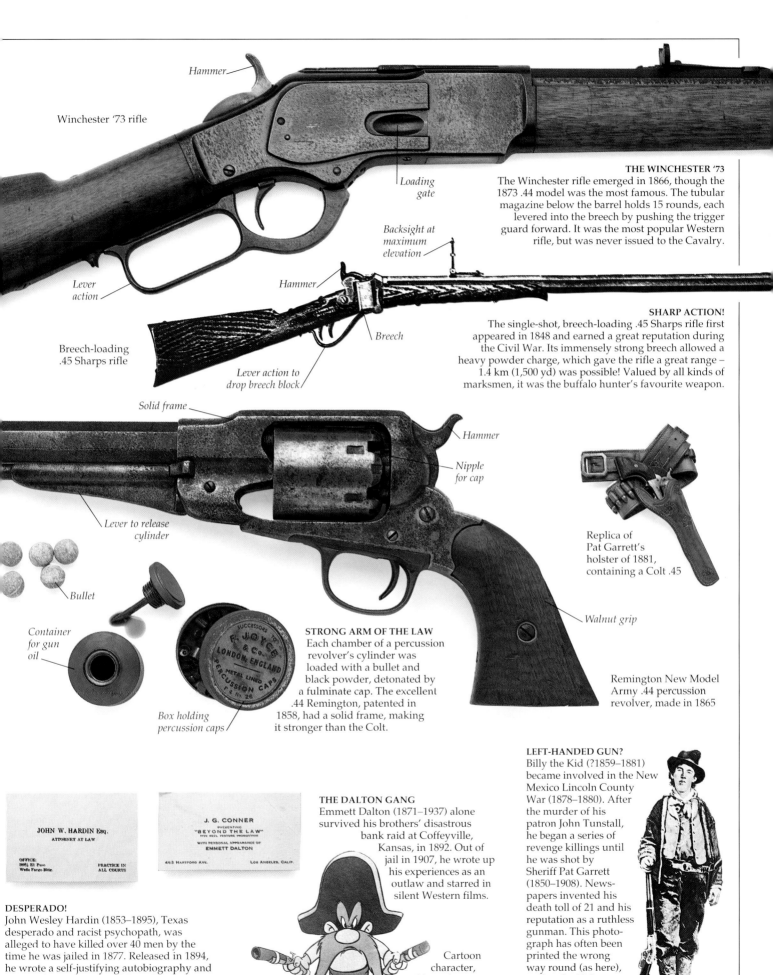

Winchester '73 rifle

Hammer

Loading gate

Lever action

THE WINCHESTER '73
The Winchester rifle emerged in 1866, though the 1873 .44 model was the most famous. The tubular magazine below the barrel holds 15 rounds, each levered into the breech by pushing the trigger guard forward. It was the most popular Western rifle, but was never issued to the Cavalry.

Backsight at maximum elevation

Hammer

Breech

Lever action to drop breech block

Breech-loading .45 Sharps rifle

SHARP ACTION!
The single-shot, breech-loading .45 Sharps rifle first appeared in 1848 and earned a great reputation during the Civil War. Its immensely strong breech allowed a heavy powder charge, which gave the rifle a great range – 1.4 km (1,500 yd) was possible! Valued by all kinds of marksmen, it was the buffalo hunter's favourite weapon.

Solid frame

Hammer

Nipple for cap

Lever to release cylinder

Bullet

Container for gun oil

Box holding percussion caps

STRONG ARM OF THE LAW
Each chamber of a percussion revolver's cylinder was loaded with a bullet and black powder, detonated by a fulminate cap. The excellent .44 Remington, patented in 1858, had a solid frame, making it stronger than the Colt.

Replica of Pat Garrett's holster of 1881, containing a Colt .45

Walnut grip

Remington New Model Army .44 percussion revolver, made in 1865

DESPERADO!
John Wesley Hardin (1853–1895), Texas desperado and racist psychopath, was alleged to have killed over 40 men by the time he was jailed in 1877. Released in 1894, he wrote a self-justifying autobiography and set up a law practice in El Paso, Texas, but spent his time drinking and gambling. In 1895 he was shot in the back by a policeman he had threatened.

JOHN W. HARDIN Esq.
ATTORNEY AT LAW

OFFICE:
2001. El Paso
Wells Fargo Bldg.

PRACTICE IN
ALL COURTS

J. G. CONNER
PRESENTING
"BEYOND THE LAW"
FIVE REEL FEATURE PRODUCTION
WITH PERSONAL APPEARANCE OF
EMMETT DALTON

463 HARTFORD AVE.   LOS ANGELES, CALIF.

THE DALTON GANG
Emmett Dalton (1871–1937) alone survived his brothers' disastrous bank raid at Coffeyville, Kansas, in 1892. Out of jail in 1907, he wrote up his experiences as an outlaw and starred in silent Western films.

Cartoon character, Yosemite Sam, with both guns blazing

LEFT-HANDED GUN?
Billy the Kid (?1859–1881) became involved in the New Mexico Lincoln County War (1878–1880). After the murder of his patron John Tunstall, he began a series of revenge killings until he was shot by Sheriff Pat Garrett (1850–1908). Newspapers invented his death toll of 21 and his reputation as a ruthless gunman. This photograph has often been printed the wrong way round (as here), so that the Kid was believed to be a "left-handed gun".

Six gun

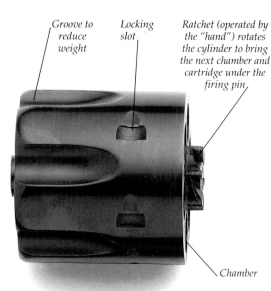

THE 1873 COLT single-action Army revolver has one real claim to fame – in the West it probably killed more people than any other. When production was suspended in 1941, 357,859 had been sold. In 1878, the .45 "Peacemaker" model was supplemented by the "Frontier" – its .44 calibre cartridge also fitted the Winchester rifle (pp. 44–45). Such large calibre pistols – heavy (1 kg, or 2 lb 4oz) to absorb the recoil – had guaranteed stopping power. The Colt was accurate, well-balanced, and could be fired even if parts of the mechanism broke, which happened often.

Groove to reduce weight

Locking slot

Ratchet (operated by the "hand") rotates the cylinder to bring the next chamber and cartridge under the firing pin

Chamber

Cylinder

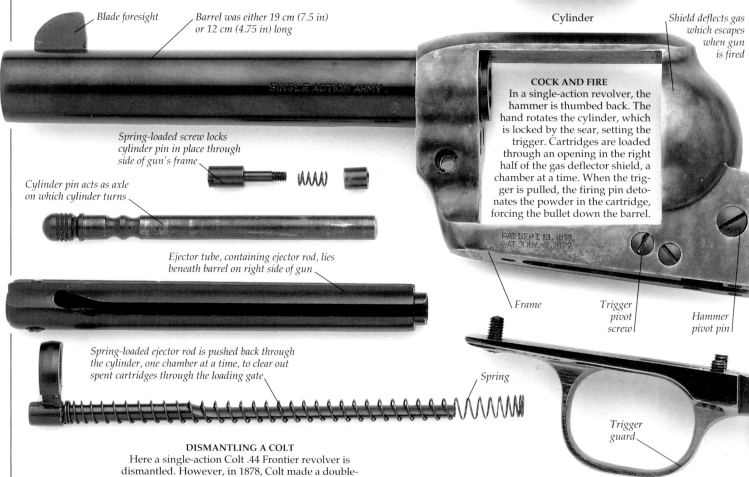

Blade foresight

Barrel was either 19 cm (7.5 in) or 12 cm (4.75 in) long

Shield deflects gas which escapes when gun is fired

SINGLE ACTION ARMY

COCK AND FIRE
In a single-action revolver, the hammer is thumbed back. The hand rotates the cylinder, which is locked by the sear, setting the trigger. Cartridges are loaded through an opening in the right half of the gas deflector shield, a chamber at a time. When the trigger is pulled, the firing pin detonates the powder in the cartridge, forcing the bullet down the barrel.

Spring-loaded screw locks cylinder pin in place through side of gun's frame

Cylinder pin acts as axle on which cylinder turns

Ejector tube, containing ejector rod, lies beneath barrel on right side of gun

PAT. SEPT. 19, 1871.
PAT. JULY 2, 1872.

Frame

Trigger pivot screw

Hammer pivot pin

Spring-loaded ejector rod is pushed back through the cylinder, one chamber at a time, to clear out spent cartridges through the loading gate

Spring

Trigger guard

DISMANTLING A COLT
Here a single-action Colt .44 Frontier revolver is dismantled. However, in 1878, Colt made a double-action revolver – the Lightning, in .38 or .44 calibre. In this type of self-cocking weapon, a firm pull on the trigger alone lifted the hammer (and rotated the cylinder and locked it) and let it fall.

TRIGGER ACTION
When the hammer is cocked, the sear sets the trigger on its spring to trip the hammer. It also locks the cylinder, so that the next cartridge is in line with the barrel and under the firing pin. Although the lock mechanism was an original Colt patent, it was notorious for breaking, especially the trigger spring.

Trigger sear and cylinder stop

Trigger spring

Trigger connected to hammer by trigger spring and sear

THE WALKER COLT
In 1847, the U.S. Army sent Captain Samuel Walker to buy Colt revolvers. Walker suggested several improvements and the new gun became known as the "Walker Colt". Though huge – 39 cm (15.5 in) long and weighing 2 kg (4.5 lb) – it was the basis for all future Colt designs until 1873.

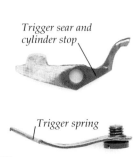

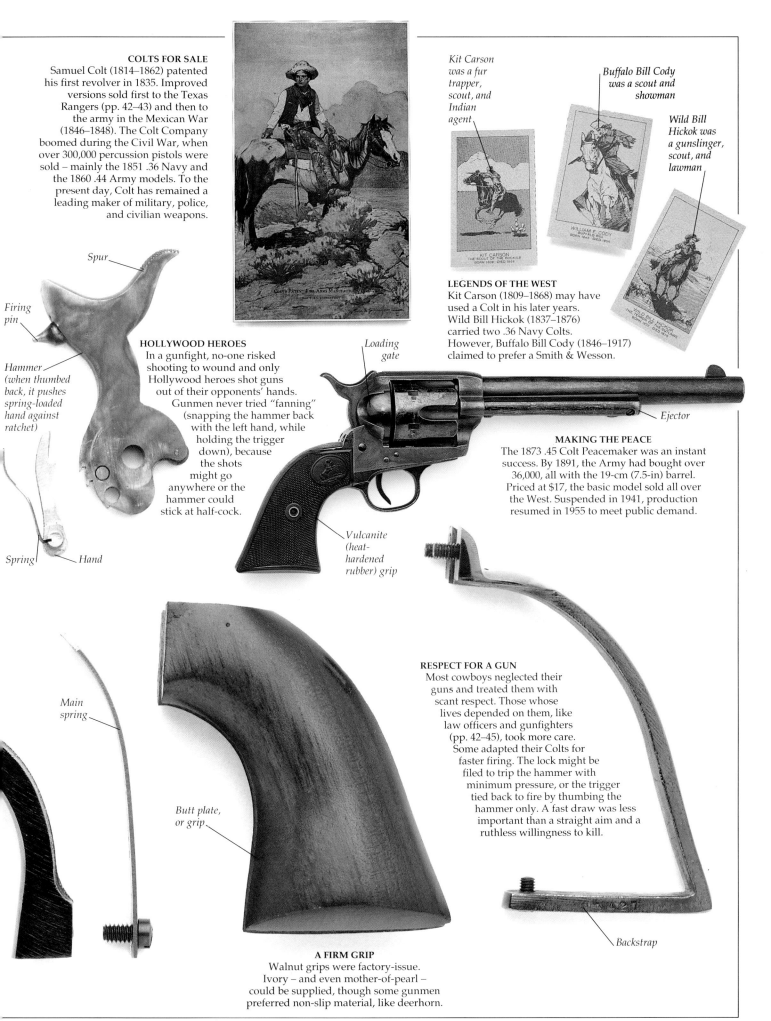

COLTS FOR SALE
Samuel Colt (1814–1862) patented his first revolver in 1835. Improved versions sold first to the Texas Rangers (pp. 42–43) and then to the army in the Mexican War (1846–1848). The Colt Company boomed during the Civil War, when over 300,000 percussion pistols were sold – mainly the 1851 .36 Navy and the 1860 .44 Army models. To the present day, Colt has remained a leading maker of military, police, and civilian weapons.

Spur

Firing pin

Hammer (when thumbed back, it pushes spring-loaded hand against ratchet)

Spring

Hand

Kit Carson was a fur trapper, scout, and Indian agent

Buffalo Bill Cody was a scout and showman

Wild Bill Hickok was a gunslinger, scout, and lawman

LEGENDS OF THE WEST
Kit Carson (1809–1868) may have used a Colt in his later years. Wild Bill Hickok (1837–1876) carried two .36 Navy Colts. However, Buffalo Bill Cody (1846–1917) claimed to prefer a Smith & Wesson.

HOLLYWOOD HEROES
In a gunfight, no-one risked shooting to wound and only Hollywood heroes shot guns out of their opponents' hands. Gunmen never tried "fanning" (snapping the hammer back with the left hand, while holding the trigger down), because the shots might go anywhere or the hammer could stick at half-cock.

Loading gate

Ejector

MAKING THE PEACE
The 1873 .45 Colt Peacemaker was an instant success. By 1891, the Army had bought over 36,000, all with the 19-cm (7.5-in) barrel. Priced at $17, the basic model sold all over the West. Suspended in 1941, production resumed in 1955 to meet public demand.

Vulcanite (heat-hardened rubber) grip

Main spring

Butt plate, or grip

RESPECT FOR A GUN
Most cowboys neglected their guns and treated them with scant respect. Those whose lives depended on them, like law officers and gunfighters (pp. 42–45), took more care. Some adapted their Colts for faster firing. The lock might be filed to trip the hammer with minimum pressure, or the trigger tied back to fire by thumbing the hammer only. A fast draw was less important than a straight aim and a ruthless willingness to kill.

Backstrap

A FIRM GRIP
Walnut grips were factory-issue. Ivory – and even mother-of-pearl – could be supplied, though some gunmen preferred non-slip material, like deerhorn.

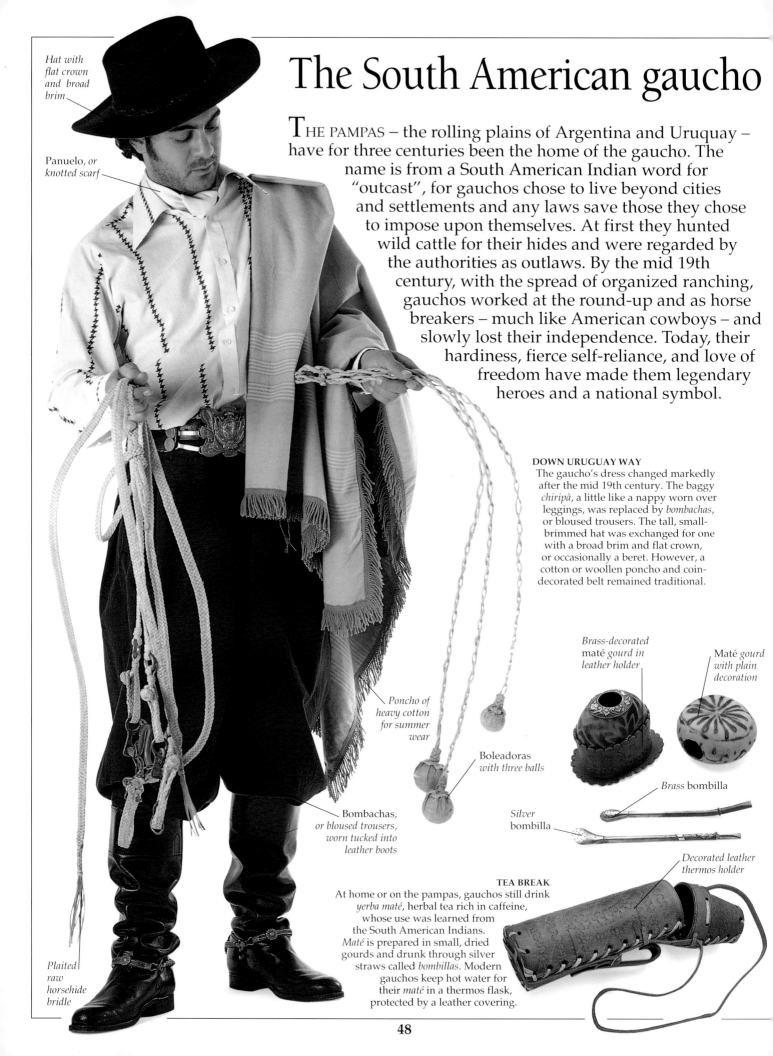

The South American gaucho

Hat with flat crown and broad brim

Panuelo, or knotted scarf

THE PAMPAS – the rolling plains of Argentina and Uruguay – have for three centuries been the home of the gaucho. The name is from a South American Indian word for "outcast", for gauchos chose to live beyond cities and settlements and any laws save those they chose to impose upon themselves. At first they hunted wild cattle for their hides and were regarded by the authorities as outlaws. By the mid 19th century, with the spread of organized ranching, gauchos worked at the round-up and as horse breakers – much like American cowboys – and slowly lost their independence. Today, their hardiness, fierce self-reliance, and love of freedom have made them legendary heroes and a national symbol.

DOWN URUGUAY WAY
The gaucho's dress changed markedly after the mid 19th century. The baggy *chiripà*, a little like a nappy worn over leggings, was replaced by *bombachas*, or bloused trousers. The tall, small-brimmed hat was exchanged for one with a broad brim and flat crown, or occasionally a beret. However, a cotton or woollen poncho and coin-decorated belt remained traditional.

Brass-decorated maté *gourd in* leather holder

Maté gourd with plain decoration

Poncho of heavy cotton for summer wear

Boleadoras with three balls

Brass bombilla

Silver bombilla

Bombachas, or bloused trousers, worn tucked into leather boots

Decorated leather thermos holder

TEA BREAK
At home or on the pampas, gauchos still drink *yerba maté*, herbal tea rich in caffeine, whose use was learned from the South American Indians. *Maté* is prepared in small, dried gourds and drunk through silver straws called *bombillas*. Modern gauchos keep hot water for their *maté* in a thermos flask, protected by a leather covering.

Plaited raw horsehide bridle

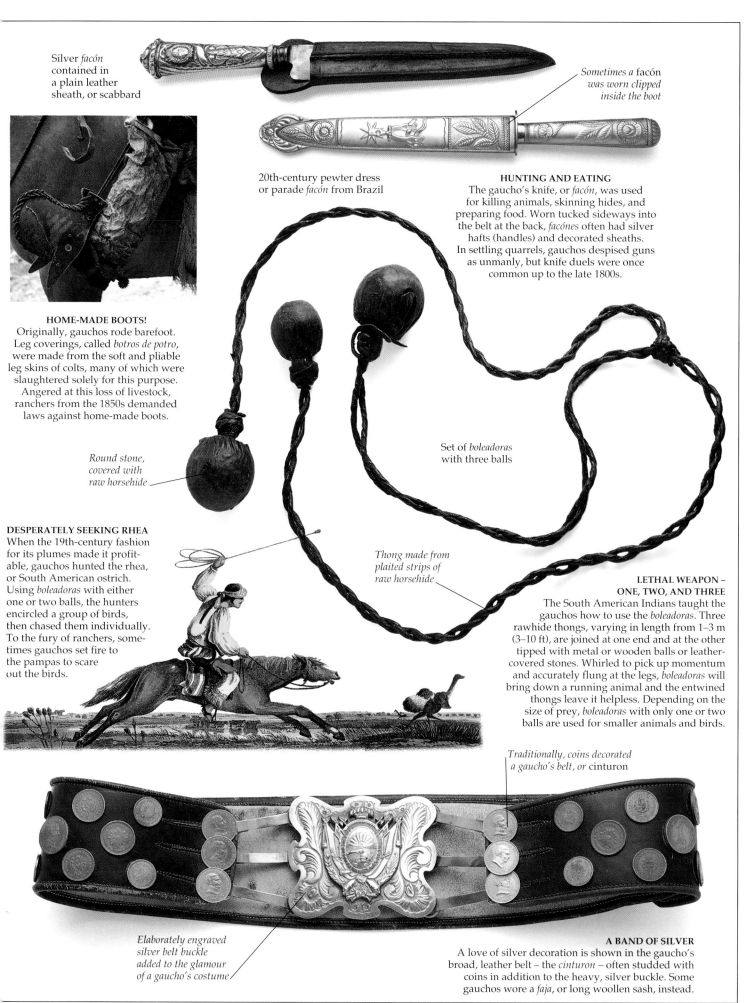

Silver *facón* contained in a plain leather sheath, or scabbard

Sometimes a facón was worn clipped inside the boot

20th-century pewter dress or parade *facón* from Brazil

HUNTING AND EATING
The gaucho's knife, or *facón*, was used for killing animals, skinning hides, and preparing food. Worn tucked sideways into the belt at the back, *facónes* often had silver hafts (handles) and decorated sheaths. In settling quarrels, gauchos despised guns as unmanly, but knife duels were once common up to the late 1800s.

HOME-MADE BOOTS!
Originally, gauchos rode barefoot. Leg coverings, called *botros de potro*, were made from the soft and pliable leg skins of colts, many of which were slaughtered solely for this purpose. Angered at this loss of livestock, ranchers from the 1850s demanded laws against home-made boots.

Round stone, covered with raw horsehide

Set of *boleadoras* with three balls

DESPERATELY SEEKING RHEA
When the 19th-century fashion for its plumes made it profitable, gauchos hunted the rhea, or South American ostrich. Using *boleadoras* with either one or two balls, the hunters encircled a group of birds, then chased them individually. To the fury of ranchers, sometimes gauchos set fire to the pampas to scare out the birds.

Thong made from plaited strips of raw horsehide

**LETHAL WEAPON –
ONE, TWO, AND THREE**
The South American Indians taught the gauchos how to use the *boleadoras*. Three rawhide thongs, varying in length from 1–3 m (3–10 ft), are joined at one end and at the other tipped with metal or wooden balls or leather-covered stones. Whirled to pick up momentum and accurately flung at the legs, *boleadoras* will bring down a running animal and the entwined thongs leave it helpless. Depending on the size of prey, *boleadoras* with only one or two balls are used for smaller animals and birds.

Traditionally, coins decorated a gaucho's belt, or cinturon

Elaborately engraved silver belt buckle added to the glamour of a gaucho's costume

A BAND OF SILVER
A love of silver decoration is shown in the gaucho's broad, leather belt – the *cinturon* – often studded with coins in addition to the heavy, silver buckle. Some gauchos wore a *faja*, or long woollen sash, instead.

49

Continued on next page

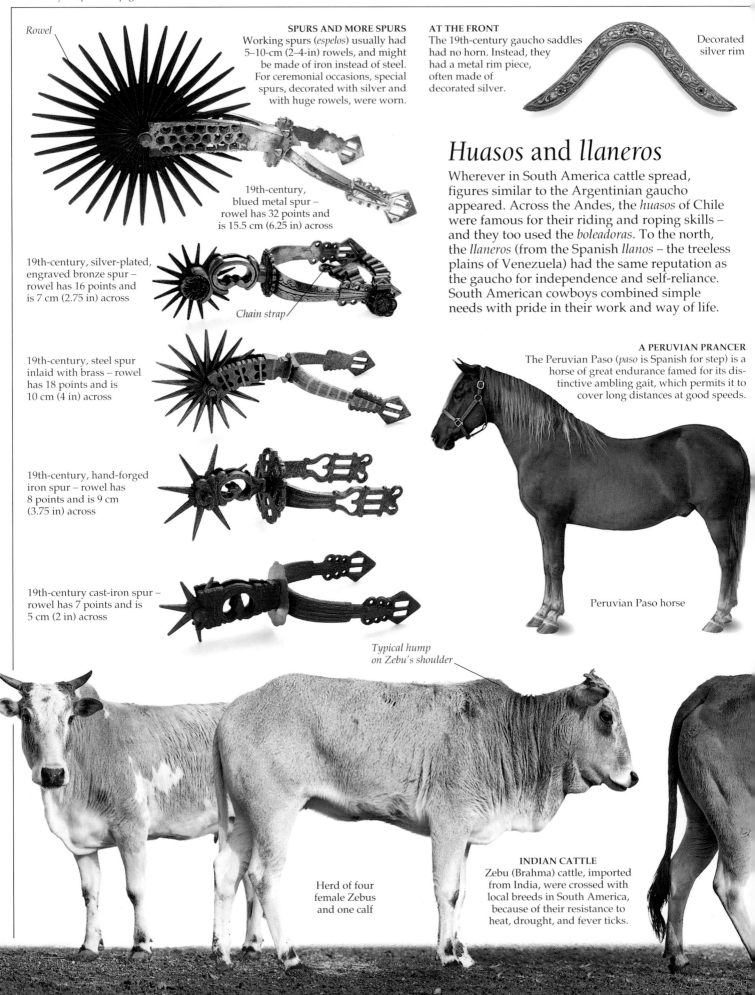

Rowel

SPURS AND MORE SPURS

Working spurs (*espelos*) usually had 5–10-cm (2–4-in) rowels, and might be made of iron instead of steel. For ceremonial occasions, special spurs, decorated with silver and with huge rowels, were worn.

AT THE FRONT

The 19th-century gaucho saddles had no horn. Instead, they had a metal rim piece, often made of decorated silver.

Decorated silver rim

19th-century, blued metal spur – rowel has 32 points and is 15.5 cm (6.25 in) across

19th-century, silver-plated, engraved bronze spur – rowel has 16 points and is 7 cm (2.75 in) across

Chain strap

19th-century, steel spur inlaid with brass – rowel has 18 points and is 10 cm (4 in) across

19th-century, hand-forged iron spur – rowel has 8 points and is 9 cm (3.75 in) across

19th-century cast-iron spur – rowel has 7 points and is 5 cm (2 in) across

Huasos and *llaneros*

Wherever in South America cattle spread, figures similar to the Argentinian gaucho appeared. Across the Andes, the *huasos* of Chile were famous for their riding and roping skills – and they too used the *boleadoras*. To the north, the *llaneros* (from the Spanish *llanos* – the treeless plains of Venezuela) had the same reputation as the gaucho for independence and self-reliance. South American cowboys combined simple needs with pride in their work and way of life.

A PERUVIAN PRANCER

The Peruvian Paso (*paso* is Spanish for step) is a horse of great endurance famed for its distinctive ambling gait, which permits it to cover long distances at good speeds.

Peruvian Paso horse

Typical hump on Zebu's shoulder

Herd of four female Zebus and one calf

INDIAN CATTLE

Zebu (Brahma) cattle, imported from India, were crossed with local breeds in South America, because of their resistance to heat, drought, and fever ticks.

Very high horn

GUATEMALAN SADDLE
This modern, 20th-century saddle is from Guatemala in Central America. Although this particular example was used by an English nurse who travelled on horseback to visit her patients in the countryside, it could have been used by a cowboy as a cutting saddle (pp. 32–33), because of its very high horn.

OLD-STYLE GAUCHO
Gauchos fought in Argentina's war of independence against Spain (1810–1816) and came to be seen as patriots, not outlaws. Though employed by *estancieros* (ranchers), they needed little and tried to remain self-sufficient. This gaucho (c. 1860) from the Buenos Aires region, wears the old-style dress.

ODD-SHAPED STIRRUPS
These triangular, brass stirrups (*estribos* in Spanish) with swivel tops probably date from the 17th century. Their shape and decoration suggest they belonged to a man of position, rather than a plainsman.

Swivel top

17th-century brass stirrups

Foliage decoration

Quirt

20th-century saddle from Guatemala

Elaborate carving

BARE TOES!
Up to the mid 19th century, gauchos rode barefoot, with their big toes thrust through the stirrups. The results were alarming – foreign visitors often made comments on gauchos' deformed feet.

A DIFFERENT KIND OF SLIPPER
Estancieros and other members of the upper classes could afford metal shoe stirrups for their wives and children. These were safer, since the foot could not slip through, and offered protection.

Rawhide stirrup leather

South American stirrups were made from either metal or wood, as in this pair from Argentina

IF THE STRAP FITS, WEAR IT
Poor, barefoot gauchos still wore spurs, which had to be attached to the foot by a leather heel strap. This spur seems something of a do-it-yourself creation – the shank has been drilled in order to have a crude rowel added.

Child's brass shoe stirrup

Lady's silver shoe stirrup

Silver keeper

Shank

South American leather heel strap, with separate rowel spur attached

Hanging fold of skin acts as radiator to get rid of excess heat

Zebu calf is 21 months old

Camargue *gardians*

A WILD LANDSCAPE of salt marshes and sandy lagoons, the Camargue lies in the delta of the River Rhône in southern France. Hot and humid in the summer and swept by the cold *mistral* wind in winter, this part of Provence is sometimes called the "Wild West of France". *Manades*, or herds, of black fighting bulls are bred by the *manadiers* (ranchers) and tended by *gardians* (*garder* is French for "look after"), or keepers, who ride the unique white horses of the region. The *gardians* have their origins in the *gardo-besti* (cattle keeper) of the Middle Ages (A.D. 500–1350) and follow a code of honour like that of chivalry and courtesy of the knights of old. The *Confrérie des gardians* (brotherhood, or Order, of the *gardians*) was founded in 1512. Many customs had faded until the Marquis Folco Baroncelli (1869–1943) revived them in the 1880s. He loved Provence, especially the lifestyle of the *gardians* which he himself shared.

HERDER OF CATTLE
This *gardian* of the late 1800s is dressed in winter clothes and tends a *manade* near his *cabane*. Usually one-roomed, these cottages had the door at the south end to shelter it from the *mistral,* that blows from the north.

SUNDAY BEST
The beautiful traditional women's costumes of the Arles region are worn here by wives of *gardians* of the 1920s. Originally from the reign of Louis XV (1715–1774), this tradition had begun to die out until encouraged by the poet, Frederic Mistral (1830–1914), leader of the movement to revive Provençal culture. Now such costumes are worn for festivals.

MODERN MOTHER AND CHILD
Today, although few of the ranch owners are women, the wives and children of *gardians* share the work with the men, tending herds of both horses and bulls. This *gardiane* wears clothes similar to the men, except for the divided riding skirt. Children help, too, and learn to ride at a very young age. This boy is wearing a waistcoat and trousers made of "moleskin" (a type of cotton). His outfit is just like his father's (right), except for the jacket.

Moleskin waistcoat

Split riding skirt

Owner's brand mark

READY FOR A PARADE
These neat spurs (right) are worn for particularly elaborate events, such as parades and festivals. They look more elegant than working spurs (below) and are less likely to startle the horse.

Parade spurs

OLD-STYLE BOOTS
These are old-style riding boots, made of leather. Nowadays, short, calf-length boots are more common, as in America. In the 1800s, some *gardians* wore *sabots*, or clogs, which had flat soles and no heels.

A pair of working spurs

A PAIR OF WORKING SPURS
Gardians wear short, steel spurs with a ten-point rowel, held on the boot by a small strap. Horses are spurred only when real speed is necessary – for example, when dodging an angry bull.

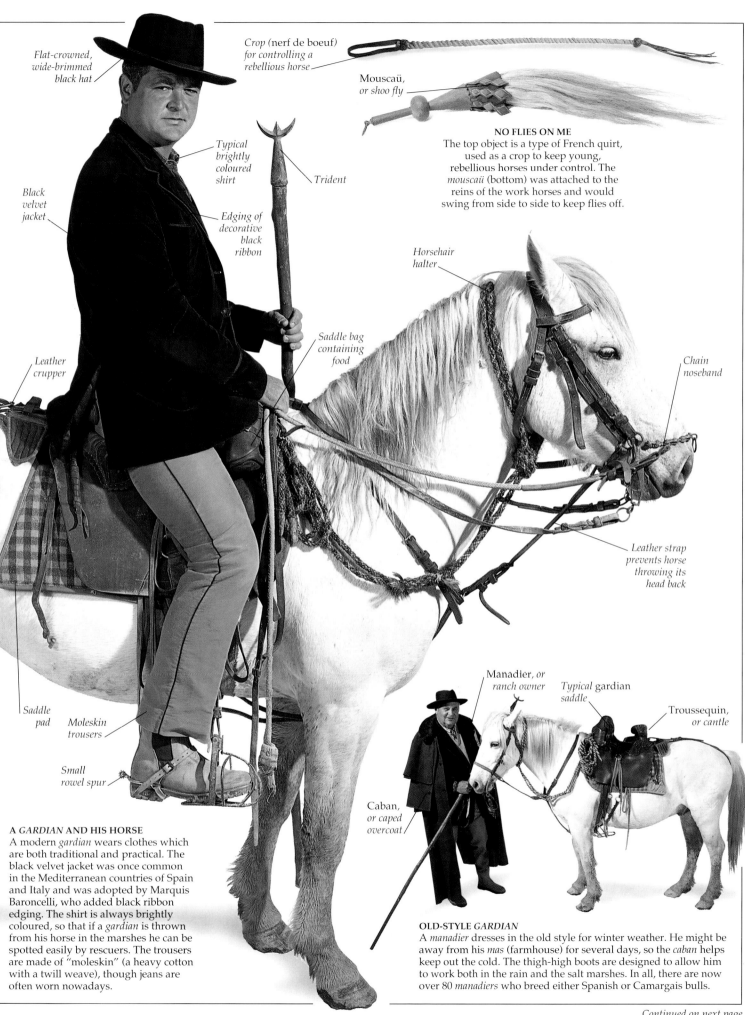

Flat-crowned,
wide-brimmed
black hat

Crop (nerf de boeuf)
for controlling a
rebellious horse

Mouscaü,
or shoo fly

NO FLIES ON ME
The top object is a type of French quirt,
used as a crop to keep young,
rebellious horses under control. The
mouscaii (bottom) was attached to the
reins of the work horses and would
swing from side to side to keep flies off.

Typical
brightly
coloured
shirt

Trident

Black
velvet
jacket

Edging of
decorative
black
ribbon

Horsehair
halter

Chain
noseband

Leather
crupper

Saddle bag
containing
food

Leather strap
prevents horse
throwing its
head back

Saddle
pad

Moleskin
trousers

Small
rowel spur

Manadier, or
ranch owner

Typical gardian
saddle

Troussequin,
or cantle

Caban,
or caped
overcoat

A *GARDIAN* AND HIS HORSE
A modern *gardian* wears clothes which
are both traditional and practical. The
black velvet jacket was once common
in the Mediterranean countries of Spain
and Italy and was adopted by Marquis
Baroncelli, who added black ribbon
edging. The shirt is always brightly
coloured, so that if a *gardian* is thrown
from his horse in the marshes he can be
spotted easily by rescuers. The trousers
are made of "moleskin" (a heavy cotton
with a twill weave), though jeans are
often worn nowadays.

OLD-STYLE *GARDIAN*
A *manadier* dresses in the old style for winter weather. He might be
away from his *mas* (farmhouse) for several days, so the *caban* helps
keep out the cold. The thigh-high boots are designed to allow him
to work both in the rain and the salt marshes. In all, there are now
over 80 *manadiers* who breed either Spanish or Camargais bulls.

Continued on next page

THE DRAMA OF THE BULLRING

So popular are the *courses à la cocarde*, or bullfights, that they are held in arenas. Some of these date from Roman times, like this one in Arles which can hold over 23,000 people. *Courses* also take place in villages, set in either improvised or permanent bullrings. *Cocardiers* are bulls that appear in the arena.

SNATCH THE RED ROSETTE

With the bull carefully secured, the red ribbon *cocarde* is centred on the bull's forehead by tying the string around the base of each horn. White tassels are attached to each horn also. Bullfighters are called *razeteurs* from *razet* (the half circle in which they must run to grab the *cocarde*). They use a *crochet* shaped like the talons of a bird of prey. There are two types – the modern (right) and the old style (far right).

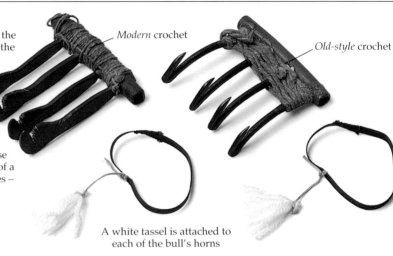

Modern crochet · *Old-style* crochet

A white tassel is attached to each of the bull's horns

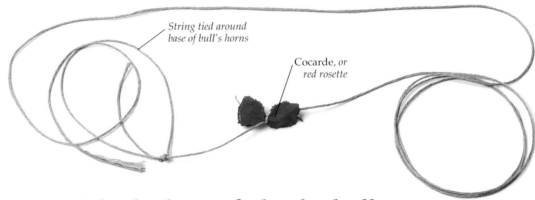

String tied around base of bull's horns

Cocarde, or red rosette

Only the brave fight the bulls

Provençal bullfights are tests of daring and skill, without the blood and death of the Spanish *corrida*. On foot, men try to snatch a *cocarde* (rosette) tied between the bull's horns, using a *crochet* (hook). A Camargue bull can charge quicker and turn more sharply than a fast horse, so the game is dangerous as well as exciting. The bulls are taken back to their *manade* (herd) when the spectacle is over. Today in the Camargue, there are around 60 breeders of the black Camargais bulls, while over 20 breed the Spanish bulls.

THE BRAVE BLACK BULL

A distinct type, the original Camargue bulls may trace their ancestry back to those of the prehistoric cave paintings at Lascaux in southern France. With black, curly, shiny coats, they are fierce and independent. Raised only for fighting, some have been crossbred with Spanish bulls since a famous *gardian*, Joseph Yonnet, began this trend in 1869.

Ancient trident

Bell for leading bull or cow

BULL'S BELL

Amid the marshes of the Camargue, wandering or injured animals may be hard to find. *Gardians* tie bells around the necks of herd leaders, both cows and bulls. The bells are made of brazed sheet metal. Different sizes and shapes make different sounds, so an owner can distinguish which is his animal.

BY A NOSE

This *mouraü* is for weaning young calves. Made of willow wood, it is fitted in the calf's nose. If the calf raises its head to suckle at its mother's udder, the wood blocks its mouth; but it will swing away from the mouth if the calf lowers its head to graze.

Mouraü – for weaning young calves

ABOUT BRANDS AND BRANDING

The *ferrade* (branding) of yearlings, both horses and cattle, is a popular spectacle. Each owner has his personal mark, usually initials or a simple symbol. The brand on the right, belonging to a prominent *gardian* family, is most elaborate, with two superimposed hearts symbolizing a mother and her sons. Horses also must carry the mark of the French Stud Farm Service (left) – a letter and a number indicate the year and order of birth of the foal.

Two brand marks – the left one is from the French Stud Service ("E" refers to year of birth, while "5" is the fifth foal of the year); the anchor brand (right) belongs to a former sailor

Brand marks of a well-known *gardian* family – the hearts symbolize a mother (outer heart) and her two sons (the inner hearts)

ON FIRE

Branding irons, which are heated in a wood fire, have longer shafts than in America. Bulls used to be tripped up on the run with a trident and branded as they lay on the ground. Now cattle and horses are caught with a lasso, made to lie down, given a type of local anaesthetic, and branded on the left thigh.

ANCIENT AND MODERN

The *gardian's* trident is perhaps descended from the 14th-century knight's three-pointed jousting lance. It is still used in the fields to drive the cattle, to turn a charging bull, or to separate the bulls, which sometimes will fight to the death. In the arena, there used to be a contest where a bull's repeated charges would be stopped by two men with tridents.

WILD WHITE HORSES OF THE CAMARGUE

These "white horses of the sea" have bred wild in the marshes of the Camargue for over a thousand years. They have distinctive wide heads, short necks, and long, thick manes and tails. Their very broad hooves have adapted to the soft, wet marshland. The 1951 French film, *Crin Blanc* (White Mane) aroused world interest in these striking horses and the Camargue.

The *gardian's* flag, made of gold embroidery on red silk, depicts St. George and the Dragon

Modern trident

ST. GEORGE AND THE DRAGON

The *Confrérie des gardians* had only 37 members at the beginning of the 16th century, but now has 350. Under the leadership of a *capitaine*, annually elected, the society (which has its festival on 23 April every year) undertakes charity and welfare work for the widows and families of *gardians*. The standard, or flag, of the *Confrérie* dates from the 1820s. Made of crimson, embroidered silk, it carries the emblem of St. George slaying the dragon.

Cowboys down under

O N THE DRIEST OF ALL THE CONTINENTS, raising cattle in Australia's vast outback has never been easy, although it has been an important industry since the 1830s. The stockman, or "ringer" – from ringing, or circling, the mob (herd) at night – has become a legend like the American cowboy. For mustering (rounding up) and droving he rode a Waler, a distinctive breed from New South Wales. The legend hides the fact that many stockmen were Aboriginals or, indeed, women, and jackaroos (trainee cattle station managers) have been joined by jillaroos. Stations can be huge. Today in the northwest's Kimberley country, they average over 200,000 hectares (500,000 acres). Light aeroplanes, helicopters and motorcycles are replacing horses at mustering. Australia now has more cattle than people – 24 to 17 million. By eating the land bare during drought, cattle are becoming a threat to the environment.

ABORIGINAL STOCKMEN
Australia's original inhabitants (the Aboriginals) were made to work on outback cattle stations in the 1800s. However, Aboriginals quickly adapted to stock work and made it part of their way of life. Since the 1970s they have been buying and running their own cattle stations.

CRACKING THE WHIP
Drovers carried guns only to shoot older bulls in unmustered country in order to gain control of the mob. The drover's 1.8–2.1-m (6–7-ft) long stockwhip was his main work tool. Made from intricately plaited leather, it cracks like a pistol shot.

Stockwhip, c. 1890s

Finely plaited kangaroo hide

Knife

Watch

Tin holding matches

Stockman's belt

Quart pot

Water bags

SURVIVAL KIT
From the Kimberley area of Western Australia, this handmade, leather belt holds a stockman's knife, tin for matches, and a watch. The quart pot (holding 1.1 litres) is for boiling water. The water bags hold 1.1 litres (2 pints) each – one for drinking and the other for cooking.

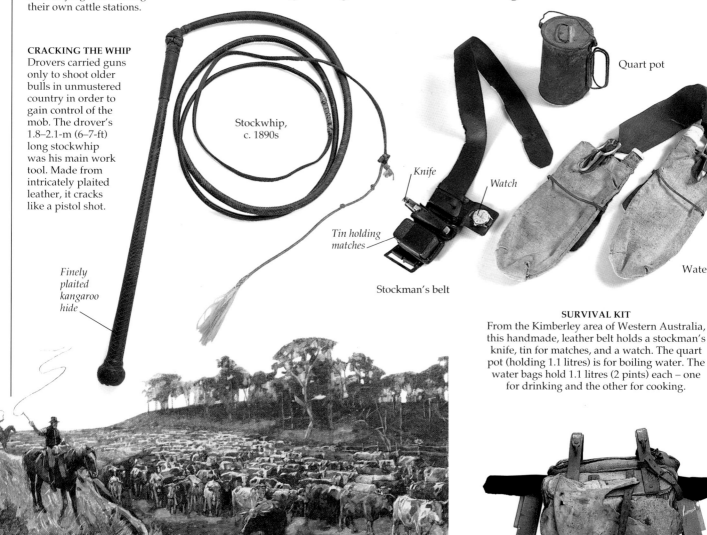

BEWARE OF THE MOB
Stockmen drove mobs of cattle incredible distances across the continent (pp. 38–39). Nat Buchanan pioneered stock routes from Queensland into the Northern Territory. In 1883, he and 70 drovers brought 20,000 Shorthorns 3,000 km (1,800 miles) to stock Victoria River Downs.

INTO THE FAR COUNTRY
For mustering and droving trips, pack saddles carried food and essential equipment. They were expected to endure long, hard use, so were made from and repaired with greenhide (untanned leather).

Pack saddle made from greenhide

Leather band on felt akubra hat

Wide wings were usual on Australian saddles (but never a horn)

Plaited rawhide quirt

Australian stockman with typical gear

Split at back of coat eases movement while riding a horse

Drizabone coat made from oiled sailcloth

Metal stirrups typical of stockman's saddle

Back view of stockman

AN AUSTRALIAN LEGEND
The legendary bushranger (bandit) Ned Kelly (1855–1880) came from the Australian-Irish community, persecuted in the mid 1800s by land laws and the police. He was a horse and cattle thief, then a bank robber. Finally, despite his iron helmet and body armour, he was captured and hanged.

THE AUSTRALIAN STOCKMAN
This stockman is dressed for the wet weather season. The Drizabone coat is a direct descendant of those made from oiled sailcloth of the 1800s. Jeans are an alternative to "moleskin" (heavy cotton twill) trousers. His akubra hat (pp. 20–21) is curled at the edge to prevent the brim buckling. Unlike American cowboys, his boots (pp. 24–25) are only ankle high and his saddle (pp. 14–15) has no horn.

MODERN MUSTERING
Modern mustering is still hard work but has become more mechanized. A wagonette brings food and many drovers ride motorcycles. Dogs are still valued, however, especially the famous Blue Heeler. Bred from several dog strains, including the dingo, they nip the heels of cattle!

Cowgirls

ON THE WORLD'S CATTLE FRONTIERS in the 1800s, women made their own contribution to taming the wilderness. Those who married worked desperately hard to make homes in grim conditions – and many died of it. In the American West, cowgirls as such were unknown until recent times, though there were some cattle baronesses, like Susan McSween, widow of one of the participants killed in the Lincoln County War (pp. 44–45) in 1878. Hollywood has glamourized the job of saloon girl, at best a brief and unrewarding career. Some women turned to crime and had their exploits exaggerated by a sensationalist press, like those of "Cattle Annie" McDougal and Jennie "Little Britches" Stevens in 1893–1894.

AUSTRALIA'S JILLAROOS
Jackaroos, those who aimed to become managers of Australia's cattle stations, have traditionally learned the business by first working as stockmen (pp. 56–57). In recent years, so too have more and more women, like these two jillaroos from New South Wales.

CANADIAN COWGIRL
Wives and daughters of Canadian ranchers came to share range work as strict 19th-century attitudes to women faded. This camera-shy cowgirl (c. 1920) from western Canada wears a cowboy's outfit, including the rather uneasy addition of a pistol.

1 FAST LADY
Once freed from social rules that denied them the opportunity, women were able to prove that they could ride as fast and as skilfully as men – for example, in the demonstration of range skills in the rodeo (pp. 62–63).

2 TOUGH COMPETITION
In the USA, Canada, and Australia, the regular women's event in most rodeos is barrel racing, which is based on the technique of cutting out cows from the herd. Each rider races her horse in a cloverleaf pattern around three empty oil drums, placed in a triangle. The fastest time wins, but five seconds is added for every barrel knocked over.

Body leans in direction which rider wants horse to take

Light touch of rein to neck guides horse around barrel

CALAMITY JANE
Martha "Calamity Jane" Cannary (?1852–1903) became famous for wearing men's clothes, swearing, and drinking. She hung around army and mining camps but, despite the legend, was never a scout nor a girlfriend of Wild Bill Hickok (pp. 42–43). Dime novelists made her a pistol-packing terror and she tried to trade on that image.

Poster advertising the amazing feats of marksmanship exhibited by Annie Oakley in Buffalo Bill's Wild West show

"LITTLE SURE SHOT"
Phoebe "Annie Oakley" Moses (1860–1926), the incredible trick-shot star of Buffalo Bill Cody's Wild West show (pp. 60–61), is remembered as a Western superwoman. In fact, born in Ohio, she visited the West only with the show. Her legend, however, was immortalized on stage and screen by the hit musical *Annie Get Your Gun*.

3 PEAK FITNESS
If the horse has to be particularly agile and in top condition to compete in barrel racing, the rider, too, must be fit. Great skill and confidence are needed for this event.

Rider's feet must be kept close to sides of horse to avoid knocking the barrel over

Split skirt

Flank muscles are well-developed to help achieve high speeds

4 ALL-GIRL RODEOS
All-girl rodeos are popular. Like cowboys, cowgirls compete in bareback bronc-riding, tie-down calf roping, goat tying, and snatching a ribbon from a running steer's back. All these events have to be performed at extreme speed.

KEEPING UP THE TRADITION
The wives and daughters of the *gardians* of the Camargue in southern France (pp. 52–55) are as much involved in the work of tending the herds of unique horses and bulls as the men. Women wear the same mixture of traditional and practical dress as the men – except for a divided riding skirt!

Cowboy culture

THE COWBOY HAS RIDDEN OFF THE RANGE of reality and into a new life as a mythical hero. This strange process was well under way by 1900, and surviving "saddle tramps" from the Old West must have been surprised. Wild West shows from the 1880s had starred cowboys as dashing men of action. Then writers created the strong, silent cowboy, slow to act but invincible when angered. From 1903, the new film industry snapped up this ready-made hero and guaranteed his popularity. So powerful is the cowboy's romantic image that it has found expression in music and fashion and has been used eagerly by advertisers. Fantasies about the man with his horse and gun, riding the wide open spaces, are a theme of the 20th century.

SMITH & WESSON
REVOLVERS

An advertisement for guns depicts the cowboy myth

DUDE RANCHING
Carrying cameras instead of guns, the dude ranchers of today try to recreate the excitement of the West without having to undergo the severe hardships endured by the true cowboy.

THE FIRST WESTERN SUPERSTAR
Tom Mix (1880–1940) made nearly 300 films and was the first Western superstar. He deliberately mixed furious action with flamboyant dress to give the cowboy a spectacular image.

Tom Mix's hat, specially designed for him by the Stetson company

Tom Mix's gun

FROM GUNS TO GUITARS
"Cowboy" singers became popular on radio in the 1920s and in sound films after 1928. Most famous was Gene Autry (b. 1907) who, riding "Champion the Wonder Horse" in 95 movies, showed a cowboy pure in thought and deed. Guitar-strumming Roy Rogers (b. 1912), the top western star from 1942 to 1954, also rode a famous horse named " Trigger". Audiences, mostly young, eventually saw that a cowboy's guitar was as important as his gun. Both stars had their own TV series in 1950–1951.

THE RISE OF THE MYTH
More Westerns have been made by Hollywood than any other kind of film. Early silent stars like William S. Hart (1865–1946) began a trend later firmly followed by John Wayne (1907–1979) – the cowboy hero as a rugged individualist doing right at the point of a gun. Since the mid 1960s, Clint Eastwood (b. 1930) has portrayed a grimmer hero in a grittier West.

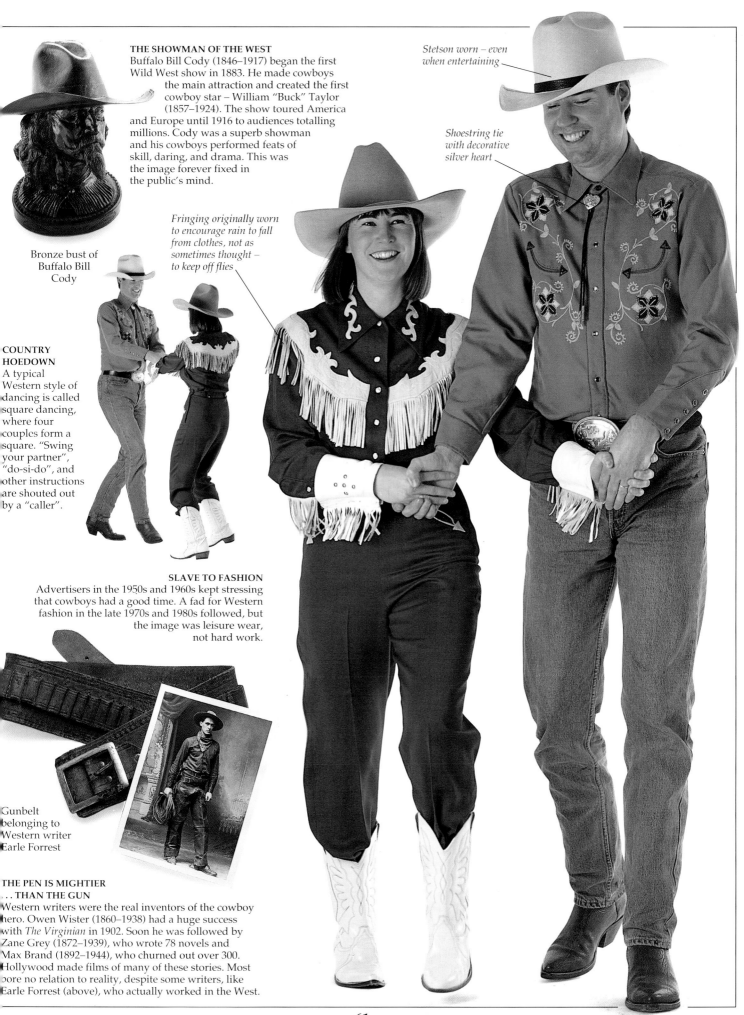

THE SHOWMAN OF THE WEST
Buffalo Bill Cody (1846–1917) began the first Wild West show in 1883. He made cowboys the main attraction and created the first cowboy star – William "Buck" Taylor (1857–1924). The show toured America and Europe until 1916 to audiences totalling millions. Cody was a superb showman and his cowboys performed feats of skill, daring, and drama. This was the image forever fixed in the public's mind.

Bronze bust of Buffalo Bill Cody

COUNTRY HOEDOWN
A typical Western style of dancing is called square dancing, where four couples form a square. "Swing your partner", "do-si-do", and other instructions are shouted out by a "caller".

SLAVE TO FASHION
Advertisers in the 1950s and 1960s kept stressing that cowboys had a good time. A fad for Western fashion in the late 1970s and 1980s followed, but the image was leisure wear, not hard work.

Gunbelt belonging to Western writer Earle Forrest

THE PEN IS MIGHTIER ... THAN THE GUN
Western writers were the real inventors of the cowboy hero. Owen Wister (1860–1938) had a huge success with *The Virginian* in 1902. Soon he was followed by Zane Grey (1872–1939), who wrote 78 novels and Max Brand (1892–1944), who churned out over 300. Hollywood made films of many of these stories. Most bore no relation to reality, despite some writers, like Earle Forrest (above), who actually worked in the West.

Stetson worn – even when entertaining

Shoestring tie with decorative silver heart

Fringing originally worn to encourage rain to fall from clothes, not as sometimes thought – to keep off flies

Rodeo thrills and spills

COWBOYS' SKILLS ARE SPECTACULAR – how natural that they should be turned into a paying spectacle. Rodeos (from the Spanish for round-up) probably began as friendly competitions between cowboys when trail herds met. From the 1880s, they became formal events and were later professionalized in the 1930s. Since 1945 the Rodeo Cowboys Association has controlled what is one of the biggest spectator sports in the USA, with over 500 rodeos annually. In Canada, the famous Calgary Stampede began in 1912 and the Australian Rough Riders Association organizes big prize meetings. The five traditional rodeo events are saddle bronc riding, calf roping, bareback bronc riding, steer wrestling, and Brahma bull riding. The first two are range skills, but the last three also show strength and daring. The Calgary Stampede has added chuck wagon racing. Rodeo is now show-business – part contest and part circus – and American rodeos offer over $15 million in prize money each year.

1 CALF ROPING
Calf roping requires both co-operation between horse and rider and skill with a lariat (pp. 34–35). The cowboy chases a calf and ropes it (he is disqualified if he misses), ties the rope to the saddlehorn, and leaps from his horse.

RIDE 'EM COWBOY!
In saddle bronc riding, the cowboy uses a hornless saddle and a single rein attached to a halter – as depicted in this painting *Bucked: A Rodeo Thrill* by Stanley L. Wood (1866–1928). The cowboy mounts the horse in a chute (enclosure) and on its release must hold the rein in one hand, keeping the other free, spur the horse, and stay on for eight seconds. Points are earned by the rider for style – and by the horse for bucking properly! In any case, it is not a pleasant experience for the horse – or the rider either, particularly if he falls off.

AROUND AND AROUND
Barrel racing requires some of the same skills as cutting out a calf from the herd (pp. 32–33). It is the traditional cowgirls' event in rodeo (pp. 58–59).

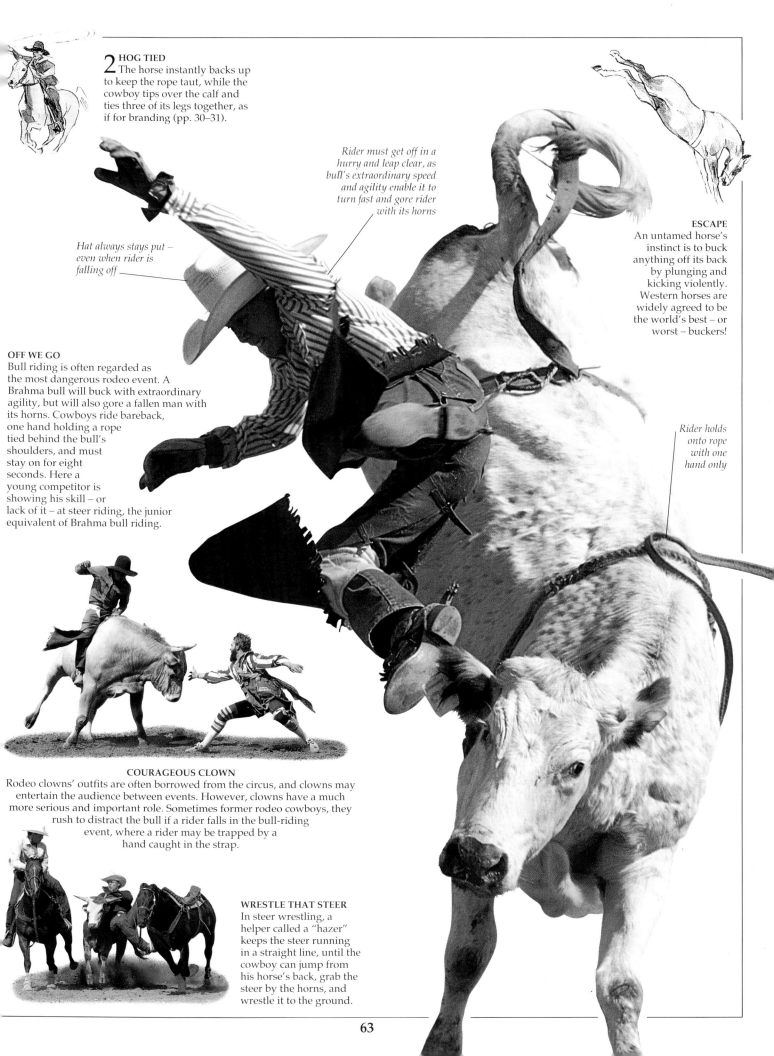

2 HOG TIED
The horse instantly backs up to keep the rope taut, while the cowboy tips over the calf and ties three of its legs together, as if for branding (pp. 30–31).

Rider must get off in a hurry and leap clear, as bull's extraordinary speed and agility enable it to turn fast and gore rider with its horns

Hat always stays put – even when rider is falling off

ESCAPE
An untamed horse's instinct is to buck anything off its back by plunging and kicking violently. Western horses are widely agreed to be the world's best – or worst – buckers!

OFF WE GO
Bull riding is often regarded as the most dangerous rodeo event. A Brahma bull will buck with extraordinary agility, but will also gore a fallen man with its horns. Cowboys ride bareback, one hand holding a rope tied behind the bull's shoulders, and must stay on for eight seconds. Here a young competitor is showing his skill – or lack of it – at steer riding, the junior equivalent of Brahma bull riding.

Rider holds onto rope with one hand only

COURAGEOUS CLOWN
Rodeo clowns' outfits are often borrowed from the circus, and clowns may entertain the audience between events. However, clowns have a much more serious and important role. Sometimes former rodeo cowboys, they rush to distract the bull if a rider falls in the bull-riding event, where a rider may be trapped by a hand caught in the strap.

WRESTLE THAT STEER
In steer wrestling, a helper called a "hazer" keeps the steer running in a straight line, until the cowboy can jump from his horse's back, grab the steer by the horns, and wrestle it to the ground.

Index

Acknowledgements

Dorling Kindersley would like to thank:
The Mailhan family (Marcel, Pascal, Caroline, Raoul, and Jacques), Roger and Louis Galeron, and Mme. Françoise Yonnet for providing props, animals, and models for the photo shoot in the Camargue, and Céline Carez for organizing the trip. Graham and Karen Aston, BAPTY & Company Ltd, The Rev. Peter Birkett MA, Brian Borrer's Artistry in Leather (Western Saddlemaker), Foxhill Stables & Carriage Repository, J.D. Consultancy (agent for J. B. Collection), Bryan Mickleburgh's American Costumes & Props, Ros Pearson's Avon Western Wear, David Gainsborough Roberts, and Walsall Leather Museum for providing props for photography.

Pam and Paul Brown of Zara Stud, Peter and Mandy Richman of Cotmarsh Horned Pedigree Hereford/Creeslea Aberdeen Angus (Swindon), Sterling Quarter Horses, Val Taylor's Moores Farm, Twycross Zoo, and Sheila Whelan's The Avenue Riding Centre for providing animals and riding arenas for photography. Karl Bandy, The Rev. Peter Birkett, Brian Borrer, Pam and Paul Brown, John Denslow, Wayne Findlay, Dave Morgan, Andrew Nash, Helen Parker, Scott Steedman, Francesca Sternberg, and J.B. Warriner as models. Bob Gordon, Manisha Patel, Sharon Spencer, Helena Spiteri, and Scott Steedman for editorial/design help. Lucky Productions S.A., Geneva, Switzerland for permission to reproduce "Lucky Luke".

Authenticators: Graham Aston, Jane Lake, and James White
Index: Lynne Bresler
Map: Sallie Alane Reason
Model: Gordon Models
Mongolian paintings: Ts Davaahuu

Picture credits
a=above, b=below, c=centre, l=left, r=right
Australian Picture Library, Sydney 58cl.
Australian Stockman's Hall of Fame 56cr, 56br.
Bettmann Archive, New York 40tr.
Bruce Coleman 36ct, 36cl, 36cb.
Culver Pictures Inc., New York 39bc.
© Dorling Kindersley: Bob Langrish 6–7cr, 13tr, 13ctr, 13cbr, 13cb, 18–19ct, 19c, 19cr, 50cr; Jerry Young 40bl, 40br, 41cl, 41c.
Dave King 45t, 47cr.
Mary Evans Picture Library 6tl, 7cr, 7br, 13br, 25br, 31cr, 33cr, 34tl, 51tr, 56bl, 57tr.
Ronald Grant Archive 45bc.

Hamlyn Publishing Group (from *The Book of the West* by Charles Chilton, © Charles Chilton 1961) 60tl.
Guy Hetherington & Mary Plant 29tr, 35t.
Hulton Deutsche/Bettmann Archive 45br.
Hutchinson Library 6cl, 12cl, 49tl.
Kobal Collection 21tr, 60l.
Bob Langrish 10bl 10bc, 11tl, 12bl, 32tl, 33tl, 33tc, 33tr, 34bl, 34cr, 58bl, 58br, 59cl, 59b, 59br, 62l, 63cl, 63bl, 63r.
From the "Dalton Brothers Memory Game" published with the authorization of LUCKY PRODUCTIONS S.A., GENEVA, SWITZERLAND 21br.
Peter Newark's Western Americana and Historical Pictures 11cbr, 12tl, 17bl, 18bl, 19bc, 20tr, 26bl, 28tl, 30cl, 31br, 37tr, 38tl, 39bl, 41tl, 41bl, 42cr, 43cl, 45ct, 47tc, 58tl, 58tr, 59tl, 59tc, 59tr, 60tr, 60cb, 60br, 63cr.
Photographic Library of Australia, Sydney: Robin Smith 29cl, 56tl; Richard Holdendorp 57br.
© D.C. Thompson & Co. Ltd. 36bl.